Why Science is Wrong About Life and Evolution

"The Invisible Gene" and Other Essays on Scientism.

✦ ✦ ✦

Ted Christopher

Copyright © 2020 by Ted Christopher
www.AuthorTed.com

ISBN: 978-1629671703
Library of Congress Control Number: 2020901397

All rights reserved. No part of this book may be reproduced in any form or by any electronic or mechanical means, including information storage and retrieval systems, without written permission from the author, except in the case of a reviewer, who may quote brief passages embodied in critical articles or in a review.

Trademarked names appear throughout this book. Rather than use a trademark symbol with every occurrence of a trademarked name, names are used in an editorial fashion, with no intention of infringement of the respective owner's trademark.

The information in this book is distributed on an "as is" basis, without warranty. Although every precaution has been taken in the preparation of this work, neither the author nor the publisher shall have any liability to any person or entity with respect to any loss or damage caused or alleged to be caused directly or indirectly by the information contained in this book.

Rev 3.12

TABLE OF CONTENTS

Preface - An Overview 5

Chapter 1 - The Invisible Gene 11
    A. Missing Heritability 11
    B. "Dudes, get back to us if and when you have something to report" 26
    C. Supporting Observations - Making Dogs Out of Foxes 34
    D. Some Additional Context and Two Possible Explanations 39
    E. A Little Perspective from Physics and Psychiatry 48
    F. What About Philosophy? 53

Chapter 2 - How Could Science Have Overlooked This? 59
    A. Unusual but Accepted Phenomena - Prodigies 59
    B. Unusual but Accepted Phenomena - Transgender Children 66
    C. Initial Taboo Phenomena 69
    D. More Taboo, Mostly From Elizabeth Mayer's Accounts 75
    E. More Taboo from Mark Gober's Upside Down Book 82

Chapter 3 - The Spirit of Scientism - Steven Pinker 87
    A. Science-Centered Idealism 87
    B. Some Existing Reviews of Enlightenment Now 98
    C. An Unenlightened Review of *Enlightenment Now* 101

Chapter 4 - Not Awakening: Sam Harris and Scientific Buddhism ... 123
    A. A General Discussion on Waking Up 123
    B. Some Conclusions About Meditation 144

Chapter 5 - Conclusions 151

About the Author 163

Acknowledgments 165

References 167

Preface - An Overview

This book presents a general case against the scientific vision of life and in parallel considers some of the consequences of the common allegiance to that vision. That vision as Nobel laureate James D. Watson wrote confidently, is that "life is simply a matter of chemistry" [Watson 2017, p.xii]. The cited chemistry (or molecular interactions) can also be thought of as the dynamics of material, and thus a common expression for science's model of life is "scientific materialism". I suggest herein that this materialism constitutes the most basic and influential modern scientific perspective. Furthermore, I suggest that materialism and the associated allegiance to it form the foundation of what could be termed the religion of science or scientism.

The book consists of four essays on contemporary scientism. The first two directly challenge the scientific vision of life and the latter two critique two popular extensions of the associated scientism.

I get started here with what this book and its essays *do not* involve.

1. This book does not invoke quantum mechanics. In particular it doesn't use the ambiguity associated with quantum mechanics (really the associated interpretations) to try to generate uncertainty about science's understanding of life.
2. This book does not resort to sophisticated philosophical arguments in order to generate doubt about the scientific vision. I don't care about the so-called "hard problem" of consciousness. Moreover, I am totally unqualified to give, and disinterested in, such arguments.
3. This book does not hype paranormal phenomena in order to argue against the materialist vision. While the book considers and acknowledges some such phenomena, short of extrapolating positive near-death experiences (in which we might assume that we are all booked for bliss in the end), the sober take on paranormal phenomena is that they appear to be rare and/or of little net import.
4. This book is not a nuanced effort. For example, given the extent of blind obedience to scientific materialism, you can readily find intellectuals anchored in scientism writing serious critiques of other

brands of scientism. One might also claim that the uncertainty between the relative contributions of nature and nurture constitutes a serious challenge to the scientific understanding. Additionally, you might take some recent reassessments of the structure of the biological tree as constituting a big deal. Mostly fighting over words and of course egos - so what?

The most important point of this book - and the topic of chapter one - is that the reliance on a deoxyribonucleic acid (DNA) basis for the specification of life and its evolution should have been seriously questioned all along and now is over a decade into a spectacular failure. That presumed DNA basis naturally provides the foundation for behavioral genetics and personal genomics, but the associated searches are failing to find anything beyond an optimistic "almost nothing". If our DNA (or genome) provides only a little of our innate individual characteristics - including our physical gender, a few disease susceptibilities, features of our appearances, and a sort of a bio-historical fingerprint - then science is wrong about life; DNA would not be "the language of life" (and good luck finding a bio-code to replace it); and this would constitute a profound mystery in and of itself.

People have argued about the plausibility of science's materialist (or molecular-only) basis for the evolution of life. These arguments have tended to suggest a need for some extra input or steering to support the existence of a life-friendly Earth; the outcome of evolution; and more particularly, the existence of humans. Thus, they suggest that the evolution of life had some additional, perhaps divine, input. I think of such arguments as essentially Evolution II. Thus the resulting spectrum of life is the same and so is its molecular-only basis. Although on the one hand as humans we are still biochemical puppets (and thus without free will or a self for that matter), but on the other hand there was something divine or extra behind our existence and DNA. It is worth noting that the reliance on a questionable DNA basis appears to be stronger in the Intelligent Design camp than it is in genetics.

I don't see much significance with these design arguments. The big question appears to be whether DNA can fulfill its enormous expectations, beginning in the behavioral realm where there are easy to find super-puzzling innate phenomena. If the current failures in the DNA searches - sometimes termed the missing heritability problem - continue, then science's materialist model of life is incomplete and so would be its support for a biochemical-only description of its evolution. There would be more to it, and of course us, and perhaps in a supreme intellectual irony, traditional religions could be onto something with some of their perspectives (although apparently not ones implying an intelligently designed genome).

The essays in this book will introduce this situation as well as critique the contemporary science-forged intellectual landscape. The first chapter or essay of the book, "The Invisible Gene", considers the extraordinary presumptions and also faith with regards to the functioning of DNA. It then walks thru some of the milestones of failure in genomic searches. This DNA questioning will be returned to in later essays as it is the central message here. The second essay, "How Could Science Have Overlooked This?", considers some materialism-confounding phenomena that have been neglected by science. These include some unusual but accepted behavioral phenomena that are highly implausible in terms of genetics. Considered therein are descriptions of some musical prodigies and also transgender children. The latter half of chapter two then considers some paranormal reports from Charles Tart's *The End of Materialism*; from Elizabeth L. Mayer's fine *Extraordinary Knowing*; some experiences of the author; and also some points raised in Mark Gober's *An End to Upside Down Thinking*. While I tend to favor non-taboo challenges to materialism, serious consideration of paranormal reports is certainly appropriate as they provide additional mysteries for the curious and also conundrums for materialism (as well as genetics).

The third chapter or essay, "The Spirit of Scientism - Steven Pinker", considers the work of Steven Pinker - in particular his 2013 *The New Republic* essay "Science Is Not Your Enemy" and then portions of his subsequent book, *Enlightenment Now*. In so doing the chapter argues that this is typical of the superficial and arrogant pitch for an idealized entity science. The extent of Pinker's confident vision facilitated the expansion of my critique into some neighboring domains. It is worth noting that you can be highly educated, a big follower of science, and also quite clueless as Pinker appears to be in a number of areas.

The fourth chapter, "Not Awakening - Sam Harris and Scientific Buddhism", is somewhat of an indirect critique of scientism's influence as it focuses on Sam Harris' *Waking Up*. Derivative of the modern tendency to worship science has come the associated appeal of science-ification, including the reframing of the religion-affiliated practice of meditation. *Waking Up* captures a good chunk of this process and is mostly nonsense. The concluding fifth chapter then attempts to tie together some of the earlier points and adds a bit.

I previously wrote a book, *A Hole in Science: An Opening for an Alternative Understanding of Life*, which looked at some problems facing materialism and, secondarily, possible explanations from the premodern reincarnation-based (or transcendental) perspective. This book's essays on the other hand, consider the gross problems facing the materialist vision and also the distortions associated with the prevalent acceptance of it. A point of overlap between this book and *A Hole in Science* is in the critique of materialism, and in particular the unfolding heritability showdown. Herein I will attempt to limit redundancy with the earlier book.

This book is written in simple terse fashion and it is not a good idea to try to breeze through it. The basic points here are significant, largely overlooked, of course heretical, and perhaps overdue. If science's understanding of our individual specifics continues to fail - as I expect it will - this would contradict materialism, as well as derail the great expectations of personal genomics and behavioral genetics. Such a DNA failure would also contradict the assumptions of one of the most sacred modern scientific/intellectual beliefs, that being a molecular/physics-only basis for the evolution of life.

I close off this rather wordy Preface with a simple example of the kind of challenges facing the scientific paradigm. A February 2014 *Scientific American* article, "Remembrance of All Things Past" [McGaugh and LePort], reported on the remarkable autobiographical memories observed in a number of individuals. The associated syndrome is called hyperthymesia. That article opened with an excerpt from an e-mail that the lead author James McGaugh had received from a woman named Jill Price:

> As I sit here trying to figure out where to begin explaining why I am writing you ... I just hope somehow you can help me. I am 34 years old, and since I was 11 I have had this unbelievable ability to recall my past ... I can take a date, between 197[6] and today, and tell you what day it falls on, what I was doing that day, and if anything of great importance ... occurred on that day I can describe that to you as well.

The authors then followed up and extensively tested Price's recall of events and her memory was eventually proved faulty in one case - the day of the week of one of the previous 23 Easters (and Price happens to be Jewish). Along the way she "corrected the book of milestones for the date of the start of the Iran hostage crisis at the U.S. embassy in 1979". During tests she:

> correctly recalled that Bing Crosby died at a golf course in Spain on October 14, 1977. When asked how she knew, she replied that when she was 11 years old, she heard the announcement of Crosby's death over the car radio when her mother was driving her to a soccer game.

Price demonstrated an "immediate recall of the day of the week for any date in her life after she was about 11 years old". Yet she also "has trouble remembering which of her keys go into which lock" and moreover "does not excel in memorizing facts by rote". The remainder of McGaugh and LePort's article chronicled their subsequent confirmation of similar memories in about 50 people. Such memories were found to be "highly organized in that they are associated with a particular day and date" and that it occurred "naturally and without exertion".

For a little relevant exercise here readers might pause and write down a year from the last decade. Next, you can then write down a month and also a date within that month. In so doing you have specified the calendar date of a day that occurred in the last 10 years. Perhaps something like April 11, 2013. Now for the interesting part - try figuring out which day of the week that day occurred on (we will go easy here and skip trying to recall the associated personal and global events). Even seemingly simple day of the week deciphering is very implausible in a "naturally and without exertion" biological fashion.

This stunning hyperthymesia phenomenon must have an explanation and given its effortless nature, scientifically that strongly suggest a DNA basis. That would mean that such people should have a specific DNA pattern that somehow fell out of our evolutionary history that allows them to be able to effortlessly recall their lives and significant events, in a date and day-of-the-week fashion. This point is followed up by the authors, who also manage to sidestep acknowledging the scientific jaw-dropping implications of these memory whizzes. This is a little introduction to the type of miracles expected of DNA and evolution (not to mention brains). I suggest that such miracles would be highly implausible even if the last decades' worth of scouring our DNA had found significant connections between DNA and innate behavioral characteristics.

The punchline here, though, appears to be that very few people - certainly amongst those educated - appear to doubt the underlying *its-in-the-*

DNA logic of genetics and evolution, and thus the prevailing logic of life. How could so much hubris be wrong? Welcome to our Scientism Era.

For those wishing to investigate profound mysteries and possible windows to deeper meaning including religious ones, I recommend turning your attention to the heritability situation. Take the remote and speculative esoterica of physics, along with the rambling diversions of philosophers, and place them on the back burner or down in the basement. Life is where the real mysteries are.

Chapter 1 - The Invisible Gene

A. Missing Heritability

A review of a recent popular book provides a nice introduction here. A professional reviewer wrote with regards to Siddhartha Mukherjee's 2016 genetics book, *The Gene: An Intimate History* [Mukherjee]:

> [This] is a book we should all read. I shook my head countless times while devouring it, wondering how the author - a brilliant physician, scientist, writer, and Rhodes Scholar could possibly possess so many unique talents. When I closed the book for the final time, I had the answer: must be in the genes [McCarthy].

The Gene is in fact a terrible book, both in its faithful message - "we know [our future is] ... in our genes" and in its excessive novelistic style which probably accounted for the very limited endorsement by scientists. With the possible exception of a paragraph on page 487, at no point does the book hint at the decade-long, "absolutely beyond belief" failures in genomic searches. While reading reviews for *The Gene*, including approximately 500 customer reviews at Amazon, I could not find a single reviewer that bothered to question the loose logic of genetics or comment on the status of DNA searches. To their credit some reviewers did break from the common science-awed stupor and criticize the writing style of *The Gene* [Sludge 2018].

There is enormous momentum behind the DNA or genetic model of life. It is of course supposed to be "language of life" [Collins]. Thus one could easily put together a large book filled with glorious official claims about the workings of DNA. From the broad claims about its presumed role as the basis for the evolution of life down to the many behavioral contributions inferred for human beings and other species, DNA has become science's bedrock explanation for life. If the author of such a book could simply obtain a number of endorsements from scientists (preferably big shots) and place them on the back cover, that book could well become a bestseller. And few would question it as is apparent in the response to *The Gene*.

To briefly further this point I provide a couple of quotes here. Here is a one from the inside cover of J. Craig Venter's appropriately titled *A Life Decoded: My Genome: My Life,*

> Of all the extraordinary achievements of the past century, perhaps none can match the deciphering of the human genetic code, both for its technical brilliance and its implications for our future. It has charted a landscape in which we will discover the most intricate workings of our species, the particularities of our own genetic makeup, and the promise of novel approaches to health and medicine that will mark a new stage in human development, one in which inherited biology is no longer necessarily destiny. [Venter].

Then from the first page of the same book is the following from Richard Dawkins, "DNA neither cares nor knows. DNA just is. And we dance to its music". This is of course supposed to be beyond question.

Scientific materialism is the foundation for that certainty about DNA's role. If all of life is simply a function of chemistry then naturally the basis for heredity and biological design must itself come down to molecules. Given the nature of reproduction and some gross connections to DNA (beginning with the male-correlated Y chromosome) there certainly is a basis for starting down the road to what Mukherjee acknowledged is the "religion of genes" [Mukherjee, p.165]. But there are also some serious question marks facing genetic reasoning. One of DNA's jobs is to provide "[t]he entire behavioral information available to the newborn" [Mayr, p.253] which in a number of cases is simply astounding. One such example relates to bird migrations. Some migratory birds have been shown to demonstrate an innate knowledge of their migratory routes and this implies a DNA basis. But is it really plausible for a large molecule - deoxyribonucleic acid (DNA) - to have been shaped by natural selection to encode for the making of a brain equipped with migratory maps or guides? On this point even the Nobel laureate James D. Watson expressed astonishment [Watson 2003].

Temporarily shelving such questions, though, it is nice to see straightforward expressions from the underlying scientific materialism. A good example can be found in a May 2017 *Scientific American* article. That article presents recent developments in technologies used to observe the dynamics of molecules (involving x-ray based "molecular movies"). In the article the authors, Petra Fromme and John C. H. Spence, provided motivation for their own work via a quote from the late physicist (and Nobel laureate) Richard Feynman, "Everything that living things do can be understood in terms of the jigglings and wigglings of atoms" [Fromme and Spence]. Those jigglings and wigglings are of course presumed to follow the predictions of appropriate equations. Together then life might be seen as a particular subset of the material universe, a subset that might be rather boring to physicists, but is perhaps of some interest to others. Such thinking is then the basis for materialism and with it the essentially uncontested claim that "Biology [is] physics" [Mukherjee, p.142].

In fulfilling its blueprint or recipe assignment, DNA is to provide the basis for inheritance and the associated variability, which were phenomena that Charles Darwin never understood [Mayr, p.89]. The prominent evolutionary biologist Ernst Mayr provided modern biology's answer:

> An understanding of the nature of this variability was finally made possible, after 1900, by advancements in genetics and molecular biology. One can never fully understand the process of evolution unless one has an understanding of the basic facts of inheritance, which explain variation. Therefore the study of genetics [and the encompassing DNA] is an integral part of the study of evolution. But only the heritable part of variation plays a role in evolution [Mayr, p.89].

DNA is thus supposed to provide the design codes for organisms and additionally the heritable subset of DNA - the elements that gets passed along in conceiving new life - should provide the basis for the dynamics of evolution. Consistent with this role, DNA should implicitly define the innate differences between organisms, both in a gross interspecies sense as well as a more intimate intra-species sense.

A reminder here is that genes consist of the subset of DNA which provide blueprints for the construction of the body's protein molecules. DNA (or the genome) also has significant content beyond the 1.5 percent constituting genes, nevertheless "genes" (and thus "genetics") tends to be overused and can lead outsiders to think that that is all there is to DNA or at least its functional role. Quite often this book's essays will go with the flow and stick with that "genetics" tendency.

Continuing, a key point for discussions here is that in specifying the details of individuals, the genome should thus specify the innate differences between them - including amongst inborn behavioral tendencies. This again is supposed to be true within a species - and thus the field of behavioral genetics - but it is also believed to be critical in a larger way [Mayr; Croston et al; Hopkins et al]. In this latter sense DNA should specify for the differences in the instinctive behaviors displayed by different species. Ernst Mayr wrote that:

> There are reasons to believe that behavioral shifts have been involved in most evolutionary innovations, hence the saying "behavior is the pacemaker of evolution." Any behavior that turns out to be of evolutionary significance is likely to be reinforced by the selection of genetic determinants for such behavior (known as the *Baldwin effect*).[Mayr, p.137].

Thus, the behavioral implications associated with a segment of DNA code should be significant to natural selections' treatment of that segment. Therefore a gene that furthers helpful behavioral inclinations in a species would tend to spread over time, whilst those furthering unhelpful behaviors would tend to become less prevalent over time. "Helpful" here implying positive contributions to reproductive success. As an artificial contemporary example, if there were a gene (or a collection of them) in the human gene pool (our collective DNA codes), that strongly influenced an individual to *not* look both ways before crossing a street, then that gene should tend to decline in frequency since bearers thereof would tend to have reduced progeny (and longevities).

DNA is expected to provide a substantial basis for the big spectrum of behavioral tendencies found among people. This should include providing gross explanations for personality differences, including those found between non-monozygotic twin siblings. As an example, if a child stood out in a family in terms of their aggressive inclinations, then the logic of genetics suggests that they are likely to have more aggression-boosting genetic codes than other family members. It is in this way that modern genetics is confidently committed to identifying such codes, including of course a number of very significant ones. In addition to some previously identified singular DNA code segments - like the Y chromosome and codes responsible for the increased likelihood of some disease conditions - the ongoing comprehensive genetic searches should be greatly filling in our comprehension of genetic contributions, and with those contributions, ourselves. Thus the genomic researcher J. Craig Venter's has a book titled *A Life Decoded: My Genome: My Life*.

Some basic aspects of DNA's heritability role can be inferred from human studies. This connection was nicely captured by the psychologist Steven Pinker who wrote that:

> schizophrenia is highly concordant within pairs of identical twins [about 50% of the time when one is affected so is the other twin], who share all of their DNA and most of their environment, but far less concordant within pairs of fraternal twins, who share only half of their [variable] DNA ... and most of their environment. The trick question could be asked - and would have the same answer - for virtually every cognitive and emotional disorder or difference ever observed. Autism, dyslexia, language delay, language impairment, learning disability, left-handedness, major depressions, bipolar illness, obsessive-compulsive disorder, sexual orientation, and many other conditions run in families, are more concordant in identical than in fraternal twins, are better predicted by people's biological relatives than by their adoptive relatives, and are poorly predicted by any measurable feature of the environment [Pinker 2002, p.46].

So that many variations in behavioral inclinations that we can observe appear to follow (biological) parent-connected patterns. While variations in innateness are often obvious, the inheritance-packaging of innateness is not so obvious (although physically it certainly can be), but this packaging has become clearer through formal studies. Pinker's statement does, though, appear to shortchange the environmental contributions to schizophrenia [Balter].

This kind of inheritance relationship also appears to hold in the arena of disease susceptibilities and thus the medical cliche "it runs in families". In some cases this connection does have an identified DNA-basis (as for example with cystic fibrosis and sickle cell anemia) but much more broadly this relationship is simply assumed. The faith in that assumption is the basis for the big expectations of the field of personal genomics. Stepping back this inheritance assumption makes straightforward materialist sense - our innate features are supposed to come from our DNA blueprints which in turn (except for the relatively small number of mutations that occurred after conception) came from our parents. This is both the logic of science's understanding of evolution and also the associated explanation for the similarities found between offspring and their parents.

But there are serious challenges to this inheritance logic and I will introduce three of them here. First, there are large variations present in identical twins although they share the same DNA specifications. The degree of behavioral agreement between identical twins is often only around 50 percent which translates to a crude similarity in a particular behavioral tendency. In the case of male exclusive homosexuality it turns out to only be 20-30 percent [Collins, pp.204-205]. Note that this sexuality characteristic is believed to be in large part binary (expressed or not), unlike personality characteristics (such as aggressive-versus-passive) which appear to be smoothly distributed. These monozygotic differences are a good counterpoint to keep in mind when you encounter some remarkable claims of genetic determinism, for example those inferred by a specific shared behavior found in monozygotic twins that were raised separately. James Watson in fact dismissed such examples of apparent determinism as more likely being coincidence [Watson 2017, pp.378-379]). Monozygotic twins really are substantially different in a behavioral sense as personal exposure can attest to.

A second challenge is that alternative explanations involving environmental influences appear to have quite limited support. Outside of specific fears and a few familial positions (like political affiliation) growing up in a family appears to contribute little to an individual's inclinations. This really comes across in adoption studies but I would argue that it is also apparent in the relatively fixed nature of our own dispositions or personalities. Together the import of these two challenges to the logic of DNA-based inheritance are succinctly captured in another Pinker quote with regard to behavioral inclinations, "identical twins are 50 percent similar whether they grow up together or apart" [Pinker, 2002; p.381]. Hence a basic mystery.

A third challenge to genetics' logic is an indirect but rather gross one (and also arguably belongs in the next chapter). That is that behavioral genetics is supposed to operate thru the influence of the genome (or DNA) on an individual's brain. Observations of individuals with gross brain deficiencies raise questions about this reasoning, though. In a 1980 *Science* article some observations by a neurologist John Lorber with regards to a group of patients who were missing large portions of their brains were described [Lewin]. Many of these patients suffered from a condition called hydrocephalus which entails an enlargement of the brain's cerebrospinal fluid reservoirs and the consequent losses in the volumes of other brain tissues. The article reported that a number of these patients were left with only about 5 percent of normal brain volume, and yet surprisingly appeared to function normally. Others in this category not surprisingly were severely

disabled (and still others with this condition might have died prematurely).
Amongst the normal group Lorber reported that:

> [t]here is a young student at [Sheffield University] who has an IQ
> of 126, has gained a first-class honors degree in mathematics, and
> is socially completely normal. And yet the boy has virtually no
> brain.

Findings like these seem to have be selectively neglected by science and they certainly challenge neural and genetic reasoning, as well as more generally materialism. A note for readers here is that in an effort to achieve brevity I have tended to take small relevant excerpts. In this case, and a number of other examples, the source is not long, is available online, and is well worth a look.

Moving along, it turns out that homo sapiens have been referred to by geneticists as a "small species" since there is relatively little genetic variation amongst us and such limited variation is typical of a species with a small population [Pinker 2002; pp.142-143]. That lack of genetic variation appears to have followed from our having been a small species not too long ago as we struggled through a difficult period. An insufficient amount of time has since elapsed for the set of DNA variations to expand much (unlike our population). Conveniently, it turns out that any two human beings are about 99.9% identical in terms of their DNA blueprints, which translates to being different in only about 3 million bases or letters [Green; Kingsley; Schafer]. In a crude sense it is akin to having us all be identical twins, except that there are some notable exceptions beginning with the gender determining (or at least influencing) Y-chromosome.

Furthermore, of additional note here is that even within the 0.1% variable portion of our genomes, there could be plenty of irrelevant junk given the haphazard workings of evolution [Zimmer]. A gross way to grasp this point is to note that some simpler species have much larger genomes than we do. The broad-footed salamander and the onion, for example, have genomes about fifty and five times longer than our genome (note this would seem to be a serious challenge to the logic of intelligent design). A more subtle way to infer the junk or neutral content is implicitly via the soon to be discussed, inability to connect variable DNA to heritable characteristics. Altogether then, amidst the oft-cited three billion human DNA letters, there is in fact a much smaller subset that should be home to the origins of our heritable distinctions.

Against this evolutionary backdrop the ongoing genome searches are supposed to identify some specific DNA codes, and hopefully with them, some useful insights into problematic heritable conditions. These searches could also offer some confirmation of DNA's evolutionary roles. On this latter point consider the following found in a 2003 *Scientific American* interview with Nobel laureate James D. Watson [Watson 2003]:

> *Scientific American*: [i]n a century, we went from rediscovering Mendel's laws and identifying chromosomes as agents of heredity to having the human genome largely worked out. Finding the double helix drops neatly in the middle of that span. How much, with respect to DNA, is left for us to do? Are there still great discoveries to be made, or is it just filling in details?

And then after some speculation:

> Watson: [relevant research] seems to moving pretty fast. You don't really want to make a guess, but I'd guess that over the these next 10 years, the field will be pretty played out. A lot of very good people are working on it. We have the tools. At some stage, the basic principles of genetics will be known be in terms of gene functioning, and then we'll be able to apply that more to [more difficult] problems such as how the brain works.

Finally, *Scientific American* asked Watson, "[i]f you were starting out as a researcher now". Watson interjected, "I'd be working on something about connections between genes and behavior. You can find genes for behaviors…". His optimism likely reflected the confidence in the DNA model; the limited extent of our variable DNA; and the quality of the then pending research efforts. Given the difficulties encountered in the subsequent genetic searches, it is likely that those research efforts have expanded beyond Watson's expectations.

The big problem facing genetics, though, has been the unfolding inability to identify the expected DNA determinants for behavioral as well as disease inclinations. Watson's above-suggested 2013-ish finish line for identifying basic genomic connections was not accurate. In fact in a 2014 review of another 'breakthrough' in the genetics of intelligence (which purported to account for a possible 1 percent in the variation of innate intelligence), *Scientific American*'s John Horgan pointed out that in a 2012 *Behavioral Genetics* editorial it was stated that:

> [t]he literature on candidate gene associations is full of reports that have not stood up to rigorous replication. This is the case both for straightforward main effects and for candidate gene-by-environment interactions…As a result the psychiatric and behavioral genetics literature has become confusing and it now seems likely that many of the published findings of the last decade are wrong or misleading and have not contributed to real advances in knowledge [Horgan].

This was a very significant story which drew little attention and Horgan was good to point it out.

The first major public acknowledgement came earlier in September 2008, when Duke University's geneticist David Goldstein was quoted regarding the outcome of thorough (or "tour de force") comparisons between the million or so common genetic variations and the inheritance patterns associated with the occurrences of common complex diseases (which also overlap some into the behavioral domain) [Wade]. It had been expected that some of these common variations in our DNA blueprints would of course be correlated with the patterns of susceptibility to common diseases (and also to other heritable distinctions). Goldstein pointed out that:

> [a]fter doing comprehensive studies for common diseases, we can explain only a few percent of the genetic component of most of these traits. For schizophrenia and bipolar disorder, we get almost nothing; for Type 2 diabetes, 20 variants, but they explain only 2 to 3 percent of familial clustering, and so on.

Goldstein then added:

> It's an astounding thing that we have cracked open the human genome and can look at the entire complement of common genetic variants, and what do we find? Almost nothing. That is absolutely beyond belief.

Note that "common" here implies that a given specific variation in the genome is present in at least 5 percent of humans. This initial and stunning result - in particular of the common variants theory in which commonly occurring differences in our DNA were hypothesized to be (causally) correlated with the common variations in our complex disease experiences - has been followed by a decade of mostly awkward silence amidst the subsequent genetic searches.

A simple example of a common variation in DNA is the Y-chromosome (chromosome denotes a large physically distinct segment of DNA code). About 50% of people have a Y-chromosome in their genome and as a result those people have male anatomy. Similarly, one would expect that some of the other variable code sequences in our DNA would be correlated to other innate differences. Note that such differences do not have to be simple and deterministic (or visible in a mirror), rather they could merely stack the physiological deck in favor of the occurrence of a particular disease or condition. Also, due to the presence of junk or inconsequential DNA sequences, not all of the variations - commonly occurring or otherwise - would be expected to have an impact.

This missing heritability or more tangibly, the missing headline, problem is a huge deal both practically and intellectually, but it is almost never discussed. In the above quote Goldstein was assuming that rare genetic variations (variable codes in the DNA which are much less common in their occurrences) are responsible for the missing heritability. Yet no significant discoveries along those lines, or apparently otherwise, have been reported in the following decade.

The above "beyond belief" quote was reiterated in a subsequent October 2010 *Scientific American* article, "Revolution Postponed" [Hall]. Another frank appraisal also came in 2010 in which Jonathan Latham and Allison Wilson of the Ithaca, New York's Bioscience Resource Project pointed out that with few exceptions (including previously identified genes for cystic fibrosis, sickle cell anemia, and Huntington's disease; and also including genetic contributions for some instances of Alzhemier's and breast cancer):

> according to the best available data, genetic predispositions (i.e. causes) have a negligible role in heart disease, cancer, stroke, autoimmune diseases, obesity, autism, Parkinson's disease, depression, schizophrenia and many other common mental and physical illnesses that are the major killers in Western countries [Latham and Wilson].

They went on to ask (in italics) *"[h]ow likely is it that a quantity of genetic variation that could only be called enormous (i.e. more than 90-95% of that for 80 human diseases) is all hiding in what until now [circa 2010] had been considered genetically unlikely places?*". Has this point been rebutted by geneticists? Furthermore, Latham and Wilson also suggested that "[b]y all rights then, reports of the GWA [genome wide assessments] results should have filled the front pages of every world newspaper for a week". Needless to say, that missing heritability coverage did not happen.

A recent and thus more significant appraisal showed up in a May 2017 *Scientific American* article, "Schizophrenia's Unyielding Mysteries: Gene Studies Were Supposed to Reveal the Disorder's Roots. That Didn't Happen. Now Scientists Are Broadening the Search" [Balter]. The author, Michael Balter described the big DNA search tool utilized, Genome Wide Assessment Studies (GWAS), as:

> scan[ning] the entire genome for differences between the disease and control groups. [They] employ sophisticated statistical analyses to pick up even small increases in the number of specific genetic variants that might contribute to disease risk.

These searches very carefully check for statistical connections between specific DNA codes and the occurrences of supposedly heritably-influenced conditions like schizophrenia. Thus in genetic jargon hoping to identify genotypes (codes) behind the phenotypes (outcomes). "Genetic" conditions are of course supposed to reflect actual genetic contributions.

These big schizophrenia DNA searches as of 2017 involved a scientific armada numbering over 800 researchers and DNA samples from more than 900,000 subjects. Balter provided a number of superficial positive reports before offering some realistic ones. In one such assessment David Goldstein, currently director of Columbia University's Institute for Genomic Medicine, commented that the C4 finding and the associated possible insight for schizophrenia represents "the first time we have gotten what we wanted out of a GWAS." Additionally, the C4 finding was characterized by one evolutionary genetics researcher, Kenneth Weiss of Pennsylvania State University, in diminutive fashion - "[e]ven if the C4 story is right, it accounts for only a trivial amount of schizophrenia" and that its significance "is debatable".

Another fitting assessment in Balter's article came from the behavioral geneticist, Eric Turkheimer, who said that "GWAS shows that schizophrenia is so highly, radically polygenic [i.e., with many DNA contributors] that there may well be nothing to find, just a general unspecifiable genetic background". I suggest here that this is effectively, 'we know that the DNA roots are there (but we just can't find them)'. This conclusion is the opposite of the confidence communicated in the *The Gene* or any genetic literature that I am aware of. Finally, David Goldstein provided an appropriately critical comment on the nature of the genetic search business in saying that "[p]eople working in the schizophrenia genetics field have greatly over-interpreted their results" and further that they should utilize "a whole lot more humility". How many subfields of the genomic search business are there where this comment does not apply? Are there any scientists or academics willing to publicly expound on this DNA deficit?

Furthermore, the aforementioned James Watson broke from his earlier optimism and similarly acknowledged the lack of genetic insight into the occurrences of mental illnesses in his 2017 book, *DNA: The Story of the Genetic Revolution*. Watson pointed out that "[t]he history of this research is full of high hopes brought low" [Watson 2017, p.391]. He also provided a fitting quote on the situation from the geneticists Neil Rich and David Botstein:

> [t]he recent history of genetic linkage studies for [manic depression] is rivaled only by the course of the illness itself. The euphoria of linkage findings being replaced by the dysphoria of non-replication [in other populations] has become a regular pattern, creating a roller coaster-type existence for many psychiatric genetics practitioners as well as interested observers [p.392].

Watson, though, not surprisingly still upholds the faith as reflected in his subsequent statement pointing that "[t]hat said, I am extremely hopeful that we are entering an era of genetic analysis that will soon take us beyond this irritating game of 'now we have it, now we don't'" [Watson 2017, p.392].

For some possible additional insight here on the heritability process I consider a simple binary model. For simplicity here let's consider conception ultimately resulting in very similar male and female human beings within an isolated population. The only innate distinctions within the two groups are found in a small subset of behavioral characteristics. The two groups then constitute almost truly identical replicas or twins. It is a limited and boring scenario but it allows for the consideration of the basics of conception/heritability, behavioral genetics, and even a bit of evolution.

This simplistic hereditary model dismisses the very long list of DNA's supposed contributions to our behavioral inclinations. That very long list fell out of the many inferences based on behavioral genetic analyses. Those inferred DNA contributions were largely derived from twin studies in which behavioral tendencies appearing to be more similar between monozygotic twins than between fraternal twins produced genetic inferences. Of note here is that among the variable portion of DNA, monozygotic twins almost completely share their specifications (some post-conception mutations could provide for a few differences), whilst fraternal twins share on average only half of their variable specifications, just like regular siblings. The simplified alternative considered here keeps the list of variable characteristics really short: introverted versus extroverted; aggressive versus passive; tending to put on weight versus staying thin; tending towards liberalism versus conservatism; and tending towards worrying versus gravitating towards laid-back. This is obviously a very small range of variation, not too mention variation that is only binary (i.e., a model person here would for example be classified either as aggressive or passive), but it allows for a basic discussion of the dynamics of heredity.

In this hypothetical population of super-similar females and males, a particular person would only be distinguished from their same-gender peers by their specifics on these 5 variable genetic elements (and of course their freckles might differ in location too). One such specification might be tending to be introverted, passive, struggling with weight, liberal, and laid-back. If we had used a much longer and more realistic list of innate attributes, then a particular specification could conceivably describe just one person. As is, though, there may be many virtual females or males in the hypothesized population sharing the same 5 variable behavioral element specification. To add some realism here you can remember that our behavioral specifics can also respond some to environmental (or experiential) factors and thus these virtual people could be distinguishable even if they received the same genetic specifications.

Now this model can be used to introduce the nature of the inheritance process. You can forget DNA for now and simply consider that each of these 5 characteristics as being determined by a coin flip. For example then a Heads might specify a worrier versus a Tails specifying a laid-back-er. This same analogy has been used to suggest that each of us actual humans 'is so lucky to be alive' since we were conceptually specified via a sequence of coin flips (and the DNA code really can be viewed as binary) that arrived at our particular variable DNA specification. Since an actual DNA specification involves a lot more than 5 variable elements you can get a sense as to why we are supposed to be feel so lucky.

The above coin flipping scenario represents conception (a sperm and an egg merging) and given the unpredictable nature of the production of a given sperm and egg cell (via the intra-chromosome shuffling of meiosis), siblings in this model scenario would likely have different 5 element specifications. Additionally, it is worth noting that if both the mother and the father are serious worriers then their offspring would also likely have a biased coin flip with regards to their status as worriers versus laid-back-ers. In fact, in that case a better analogy might even be a one-sided coin whereby the resulting conceived of female or male would be a guaranteed worrier (for simplicity here I am ignoring a number of details like recessive versus dominant genetic contributions). In this way the behavioral status of the mother and father can really skew the coin flipping business representing conception. That skewing can in turn be seen as establishing the inheritance patterns that we can observe around us (again rather blatantly with regard to appearance). An aggressive mother and father are more likely to have aggressive offspring.

Moving onto some consideration of evolution you can think about a scenario in which the super-similar human population encounters a very long stretch of easy living (think a century or two here). Perhaps under such idyllic conditions laid-back-ers would be better suited to the survival and reproduction business and they then might produce more offspring. Note, we are not going to worry about possibly excessive population growth in this scenario. Continuing, the worrier crew might be compromised by their worrying tendency and perhaps then in someway could be akin to workaholics struggling on a long pleasant vacation. For them easy is problematic and as a result they might have fewer offspring in part, perhaps, because they would be less attractive as mates in this scenario. This would be an example of a small evolutionary dynamic, here in which a populations' gene pool gets skewed in favor of a laid-back genetic behavioral specification (officially such a dynamic is termed microevolution).

Before tackling the missing heritability aspect here I pause to reflect on some related matters. For some people it might seem that I am undervaluing the nurture aspect here. Perhaps then nurture is the big reason that "[a]n aggressive mother and father are more likely to have aggressive offspring" or more relevantly a hypothesized worrier person mostly reflects the worry-prone environment they were raised in. One can see the official scientific response to such thinking - including the limited impact of adoption on adoptees' inclinations - but I see this quite a bit in terms of my own experiences. When I look around and note the basic behavioral attributes of people that I have known, what tends to standout is the relatively fixed nature of those attributes. I can imagine either of my brothers significantly changing their appearances (hopefully not involving weight gain), but actually changing their personalities is much harder. In my experience those aspects are quite fixed.

Continuing with the innateness or nature argument, my first introduction to the nature-versus-nurture terrain was in the physical realm of athletic ability. Growing up I enjoyed a pretty physically active agenda and in so doing became aware that I was of middling athletic ability. On the other hand I encountered a few individuals, including my best school friend in first through third grades, for whom excelling at athletics came easily. Furthermore, these kinds of aptitudes tended to stick (I never exceeded middling athletic achievement).

Now back to the missing heritability problem. So what constitutes that problem in this simplistic scenario? It is the ongoing inability to find the coins which are presumed to provide a physical basis for heredity. In order to confirm the modern understanding of life, science needs to find the DNA-coins or be faced with a very large mystery. Additionally, a conceptual difficulty associated with the existing DNA model is that it is supposed to be haphazard in nature. As such, that model might seem to allow for big singular contributions like the long ago mutation believed to have occurred in the primate lineage which improved color vision. The subsequent evolutionary success of that mutation appears to have given almost all of us relatively good color vision. Yet on the other hand, complex behavioral characteristics - including elaborate instinctive behaviors and also characteristics like intelligence - seem to require something more than the haphazard hand of natural selection. That such behaviors could have shown up in DNA via evolution is surprising. That such a dynamic would not have left some significant (i.e., non-tiny) DNA contributors - which should have already been found - is extremely surprising.

B. "Dudes, get back to us if and when you have something to report"

A significant genetics research finding hit the press in the summer of 2019 and it reflected the outcome of a large study considering the DNA contributions to homosexual behavior. That study and its findings were described in a *New York Times* article, "Many Genes Influence Same-Sex Sexuality, Not a Single 'Gay Gene'", by Pam Bullock [Bullock]. An accompanying article, "What Genetics Is Teaching Us About Sexuality", was a commentary by two relevant researchers one of whom was involved with the research project [Phelps and Wedow]. Those researchers were biologist Steven M. Phelps of the University of Texas at Austin, and project researcher, sociologist and geneticist Robbee Wedow of M.I.T and Harvard. Both of these men are gay and thus had some personal interest in the findings.

The research described in the two articles might be described as sort of a peak effort by humanistic science. It was a huge and carefully done study and Bullock's article pointed out, "[e]xperts widely agree that the research was conducted by first-rate scientists" and also it was given a big thumbs up by a relevant researcher at University of Oxford, Melinda Mills, who concluded that "if somebody[s] was going to do it, I'm glad they did it.". The researchers not only plunged into the relevant scientific (mostly statistical) analysis, they also labored rather intensively to put together a sensitive presentation of their findings (furthermore some researchers even rejected the rationale for the study). Also of some note is that trans individuals were not included in the study. As provided in Bullock's article the principal finding of the study, which was based on almost a half a million paired individual behavioral reports and genomes (thus making it the largest of its kind), was that:

> genetics does play a role, responsible for perhaps a third of the influence on whether someone has same-sex sex. The influence comes not from one gene but many, each with a tiny effect - and the rest of the explanation includes social and environmental factors - making it impossible to use genes [alone] to predict someone's sexuality.

By the end of this quote the reader might feel a little irritated. Likewise, in the article by Phelps and Wedow it is stated that "while biology shapes our most intimate selves, it does so in tandem with our personal histories - with idiosyncratic selves that unfold in larger cultural and social context". Again it seems like more hedging at play beginning with a reference to our "idiosyncratic selves".

Nonetheless these reports are essentially billed as big genetic success stories. Still you might wonder what constituted success? It seems quite ambiguous with its stated conclusion involving many genes "each with a tiny effect". The comments (and for brevity Reader Picks ones) accompanying these articles are somewhat telling. First, as appears somewhat common, many (presumably well-educated) *Times'* readers seem to simply nod their heads to scientific findings and perhaps second them with everydayisms like its "[n]ot surprising really" and "[g]enes and environment matter". Additionally, there was a critical theme running through some of the comments to the effect that 'enough with the PC-sensitivities, just give us the facts!'. All of the sensitivity gauntlets that had to be run through before doing the study and then presenting the findings really bothered some readers.

But the real skinny was found in some blunt points made in the Reader Picks comments for the Phelps and Wedow article. One of these read:

> [t]his research clearly shows that there is no straight answer - pun unintended. If looking into the DNA of 500,000 people didn't help, what will?

That reader then went on to question efforts to try to understand who we are. Then another reader got a bit animated:

> [l]ess than 1% of variation!
>
> I almost choked on my pork and beans when I read that.
>
> Less than 1% of variation is risible, not even the beginnings of understanding the phenomenon.
>
> Dudes, get back to us if and when you have something to report.

I appreciated the frankness (and fun) of this last comment but must now let Bullock's article speak for itself. After going thru some generalities the article provided the skinny:

> [r]esearchers specifically identified five genetic variants present in people's genomes that appear to be involved. Those five comprise less that 1 percent of the [inferred] genetic influences, they said.

And when the scientists tried to use genetic markers to predict how people in unrelated data sets reported their sexual behavior, it turned out to be too little genetic information to allow prediction.

'Because we expect the sum of the effects that we observe will vary as a function of society and over time, it will be basically impossible to predict one's sexual activity or orientation just from genetics," said Andrea Ganna, the study's first author, whose affiliations include the Institute of Molecular Medicine in Finland.

The final bit about varying over time and societal aspects is simply a dodge on the situation. In fact, Mr. "Dudes" accurately pointed out that they really didn't find anything. For additional context, though, Mr. Dudes (technically Dr. Dudes) also asserted a mocking "[h]ello, all behavior is influenced by DNA". To which one might respond "Hello Mr. Dudes, all behavior is supposed to be influenced by DNA but that certainly is not what research is revealing". Are there any analogous behavioral genetic studies that have actually identified significant DNA origins?

Now a possibly legitimate reason they didn't find anything is because they chose quite a subtle characteristic to try to interpret via genetics. They were looking for a DNA connection to those who had answered affirmatively to the question about "whether [one had] ever had sex with a same-sex partner, even once". But is it realistic to expect a significant genetic connection with this? Likewise, geneticists might realistically expect some kind of DNA basis for a person being a liberal versus a conservative. But is it also reasonable to expect a connection for crossing over ideologies (or parties) in a single case? The real backdrop of failure here is that they have not already identified significant DNA contributors for those with reversed sexual orientation (i.e., those "born this way"). Such DNA contributions should certainly exist in order to provide the basis for such transformed orientations (as given by the dictates of genetic logic). In this particular study, by looking at about a half million behavioral reports and the associated genomes their analysis should certainly have seen corresponding statistical blip(s) reflecting the very high likelihood that individuals with innate homosexual-engendering DNA would have reported same-sex sex. There could well be different DNA specifications corresponding to the female and male reverse-sexual orientation contributions, but nonetheless the born-this-way blips should have been there.

Continuing, the article mentions possible overlap with the genetics of mental illnesses including schizophrenia. Somehow the nominal success of their genetic investigation into same-sex sex found overlap with the genetics of mental illnesses. This of course triggered some sensitive discourse in the article. But it simply highlights the real crisis facing genetics - they can't find significant connections for any of these phenomena (or seemingly much of anything). The undercurrent of the article relates to its efforts at being sensitive about possible ramifications of their genetic findings for homosexuality when in fact the real tension going on - beginning within the researchers themselves - relates to their inability to find anything. These researchers want to find something if only to experience some work satisfaction and also vindicate the basis of their profession.

The above same-sex sex study was part of a recent wave of studies which had purported to breakthrough and find some significant genetic connections. Earlier in 2018 there were several purporting to find DNA origins for educational attainment and also, indirectly, intelligence. The apparent key to this recent wave of studies was getting data for large numbers of individuals and also some improvements in data processing techniques. As expressed in a 2019 *Molecular Psychiatry* article, "Genomic prediction of cognitive traits in childhood and adolescence" [Allegrini *et al*]:

> Progress in predicting cognitive traits from inherited DNA variants has been rapid in the past five years and especially in the past year. Three methodological advances have mainly been responsible for this progress: increasingly large genome-wide association (GWA) studies, genome-wide polygenic scores (GPS) and multivariate analytic tools. The key has been the recognition that the largest associations are extremely small, accounting for less than 0.05% of the [trait] variance. To achieve sufficient power to detect such small sizes, samples in the hundreds of thousands are needed before GWA studies can begin to detect these tiny effects. Because the largest associations are so small, useful predictions of individual differences can only be made by aggregating the effects of thousands of DNA variants in GPS. The third advance is the development of genomic methods that leverage genetic correlations between traits to boost power for variant discovery and polygenic risk prediction.

As always in reading these reports one has to be leery of their inevitable optimism, but the basic idea is that individual genetic contributions are now being assumed to come in such tiny doses that to detect significant overall genetic import (to say make someone notably more likely to encounter a particular condition) it is necessary to look at many people's genomic and trait outcomes, and then to carefully process that big data collection. The resulting processing allows researchers to piece together a big summation formula that can be used to predict the overall genetic contribution for a particular trait given an individual's genome specifics. That genome-wide polygenic score (or prediction) then is supposed to reflect the many small trait-associated genetic variant contributions. The inter-trait statistical methodologies will not be discussed here.

Having not found the expected DNA origins (or at minimum, significant origins) for many heritable characteristics via earlier studies, many researchers have decided that those origins have to be hiding in smaller contributions which in turn demands very large studies. That such big (net) genetic contributions would then be hiding amongst so many tiny contributors is striking and in obvious contradiction to the previously identified single genetic variant-driven conditions. Nonetheless, that is where genetic logic (and confidence) has apparently steered much contemporary research.

With regards to one such study, a 2018 *Genetics* paper, "Accurate Genomic Prediction of Human Height" [Lello *et al*], reported on a pair of significant findings. Lello *et al* had primarily searched thru the United Kingdom's (UK) Biobank (as did the earlier considered same-sex sex study), and then using almost 500,000 individual data sets they computed genetic predictors including those for height and also educational attainment. In this the authors appeared to neglect characterizing the likely distinction for the genetic contribution to height. As apparent in the very similar appearances of monozygotic twins, physical attributes like height do seem consistent with genetic logic. The same DNA blueprints are coincident with very similar physical outcomes. This appearance connection may well account for quite a bit of people's intuition about genetics. In the case of height the estimated correlation between separated-at-birth monozygotic twins was 0.86 [Bouchard *et al*]. Additionally, a recent estimate for the general heritable contribution to height is 79% (with the remaining 21% of the variance attributed to environmental factors).

Readers can note that in describing variations in traits, this book will often use the everyday term "variation". In reality, though, the statistically-defined entity "variance" is used by researchers as above in characterizing the relative influences on human height. Another statistical note here is that variance is closely related to the quantity correlation.

The results of Lello *et al*'s study included claims of being able to predict about 40 percent of the variance in individuals' heights. In a more concrete fashion the authors claimed that the "actual heights of most individuals in validation samples are within a few centimeters of the prediction" (which from their graph appears to be roughly plus or minus a couple of inches). Given the cumulative nature of height and the fact it is a shared feature among many species, one might reasonably expect that there would be numerous DNA contributions. In fact the authors reported using upwards of about 20,000 genetic variants to form their height predictor. They also felt that their 40 percent success rate was roughly inline with the limits of their analysis. There is reason to believe that their large search pool of common DNA variants is still missing out on some significant rare variants (each of which might only show up in a small number of people's genomes). In any case, Lello *et al* exhibited confidence that they were successfully finding the expected (common variant) DNA origins relevant to determining an individual's height.

The other finding of interest here is Lello *et al*'s genetic predictions for the attribute educational attainment. Some traits that are simple and routinely recorded like educational attainment are quite amenable to genetic assessment studies. It is worth noting that such traits are quite loose in their implications, though. A very wide range in educational accomplishment can be associated with the nominal attainment of being a high school graduate (this point will be touched on again in Chapter 3). Nonetheless, Lello *et al* reported identifying a genetic basis for educational attainment which appeared to predict about 9 percent of its variability. A number of other large concurrent studies also targeted educational attainment and with it indirectly, intelligence (including [Lee *et al*, Allegrini *et al*, Plomin and Stumm]). Due to rough correlations apparent between educational attainment (and a few other commonly recorded attributes) and intelligence, you can take a stab at estimating IQs using other measures.

What I would suggest here, though, is that the polygenic findings associated with height prediction may be qualitatively different from the cognitive predictions. When people use thousands of variants to come up with roughly a 40 percent explanation for the variation in height, that should probably be taken much more seriously than analogous efforts to obtain 10 percent or so of the variation in educational attainment and with it intelligence. These large efforts involving many small contributors are fraught with possible errors and thus perhaps 10 percent is still in the shadow of error (or noise) phenomena.

One possible source of errors in these large polygenic studies is population stratification. Human beings of course are somewhat aligned into separate groups. Such groups really do have their own particular DNA variants or markers which is how DNA-based individual histories can be created at companies like ancestry<dot>com. Where this can present a challenge is when genetic researchers are trying to differentiate people based on their genetic propensities. They obviously do not want to declare simple genetic markers based on group history to be significant to a trait when they aren't. One simple example I have seen given the literature is with regards to the ability to eat with chop sticks. Naively researchers attempting to uncover some genetic determinants for such facility might inadvertently uncover genetic markers for having East Asian ancestry. The general point here is that groups really can differ in their trait characteristics independently of any genetic basis (this can of course be significant to a trait like education attainment). It can turn out to be tricky problem to normalize genetic search results by possible interference from this population stratification [Young].

Continuing with the consideration of polygenic scores it turned out that in 2019 serious complications with these studies were encountered. Some earlier studies attempted to uncover the evolutionary genetic dynamics underlying the fact that northern Europeans tend to be taller than southern Europeans. Initial analyses were positive in that genetic contributors were apparently discovered. Two later works, though, in applying those findings to the larger and more homogenous UK Biobank data set did not corroborate this [Berg *et al*, Sohail *et al*]. The new data set (which still obviously involved adults of various heights) produced somewhat different estimates for the small contributions of genetic variants found in the earlier study. When subsequently run through the polygenic score algorithm those adjusted variant scores produced overall height predictions which contradicted the earlier studies' claimed genetic basis for northern Europe's taller populations.

Based on the two contradictory study findings an April 2019 *Genomics* article, "New Turmoil Predicting the Effects of Genes" was produced [Cepelewicz]. That article's conclusions strongly suggested that the polygenic successes thus far had been unknowingly tainted by complications including population stratification. One researcher, Nick Barton of the Institute of Science and Technology Austria, said:

> [t]he whole thing is tricky, because the origins of genetic variation in any population are really complicated. Now you really can't take at face value any of these methods over the last four or five years that use polygenic scores.

One researcher, Shamil Sunyaev of Harvard Medical School, commented that "no one realized how big of a problem" the genetic population phenomena was. Another researcher commented that "[i]t's fairly humbling to see all of that work go away".

One early warning sign with regards to the polygenic accuracy was that their prediction performances varied by group. In fact, for a group of African Americans considered their educational attainment predictor failed. Some of the early reports tended to rationalize such group differences as making environmental sense, but that is doubtful. Should variations in cognitive characteristics really have group-dependent genetic origins?

In reviewing thru the polygenic score situation I encountered the work of a retired psychiatrist, Steve Pittelli [Pittelli blog] and [Pittelli]. Pittelli has apparently been following the genetic revolution from the psychiatry neighborhood for years. He claims to have spent years observing what I think of as the cycle of genetic breakthroughs. One publicized breakthrough followed by another, with little mention of their contradictions and discontinuity. Significantly, this cycle offers a superficial ongoing veneer of genetic successes. In the world of psychiatry Pittelli observed that the promise of genetics was pretty much uncritically accepted and this greatly displaced other aspects of the field's work. Pittelli in a beautifully written essay in *Logos* - nominally focused on reviewing Robert Plomin's book *Blueprint: How DNA Makes Us Who We Are* - Pittelli covers a very big swath of the contemporary genetics tsunami and its under-appreciated dangers. His coverage is not akin to the somewhat routine efforts to brace against genetic determinism (i.e., 'it is not all in the genes!') which even geneticists now conveniently embrace. Pittelli has bothered to follow the cycle of contradictory breakthroughs to their likely conclusion - DNA is striking out as a cognitive prediction vehicle in a very big way, in particular in the area of mental health. He also bothers to identify the absurdity of having roughly half of an individual's behavioral trait outcome being accepted as the result of some imagined unique environmental experiences (in the literature this is referred to as the third law of behavioral genetics). If known environmental contributors are of such limited influence, and monozygotic twins show little divergence via separate upbringings, then how much of a basis does the commonly accepted unique environmental factor really have?

What is noteworthy here is that Steve Pittelli has done a marvelous job of questioning cognitive genetics, all the way down to writing to relevant journals with his findings. And in a nutshell where does all of this lead? To a beautifully written, largely ignored essay in *Logos* (a journal of modern society & culture). I could easily use many of his quotes here but would suggest that interested readers just read his 5 page essay for themselves [Pittelli]. You might consider this sort of a warmup to chapter 3's rebuttal of the proclamations of Steven Pinker.

C. Supporting Observations - Making Dogs Out of Foxes

In Steve Pittelli's just described critical analysis, he asserts that DNA connections to intelligence and illnesses like schizophrenia and depression really seem unrealistic (in fact he deemed them an imagined "tickling" effect). Pittelli's analysis, though, did not make connections to the larger DNA vision. Such DNA-based tickling is also supposed to be involved in a very wide range of disease susceptibilities and moreover such influences are also expected all around the animal kingdom. In fact DNA is supposed to be the language of life and failures in personal genomics and behavioral genetics contradict that general role.

To see some basis for biologists' confidence in the genetic model of inheritance (beyond simple faith in materialism), you can look up an article in the aforementioned May 2017 issue of *Scientific American*. That issue contains an article "How to Build a Dog" presenting the findings from a unique six-decade long experiment involving the selective breeding of foxes [Trut and Dugatkin]. As reported by the authors, Lyudmila Trut and Lee Alan Dugatkin (the former had long involvement in the experiment), this Siberian-based effort was initiated in an attempt to grossly replicate the historical process that transformed some wolves into dogs. Lyudmila Trut's work began in 1958 when she joined the just beginning domestication experiment in Novosibirsk, Siberia. The experiment's leader was Dmitri Belyaev and they followed a process of:

> [g]eneration after generation, we would selectively breed those foxes that interacted in the most positive ways with humans. If such a process worked as we thought it would, domestication -

perhaps akin to the transformation that occurred to turn wolves into dogs - would unfold before our eyes.

Belyaev's idea was that the key selection criteria for the historical domestication process had been tameness, and that is what his group aimed to follow with their foxes. He also felt that:

> what we now call the domestication syndrome - curly tails, floppy ears, mottled fur pattern, the maintaining of juvenile facial characteristics (roundness and blunted snout) into adulthood, and less reliance on seasonal breeding - were by-products of selecting for the tamest animals.

The Novosibirsk experiment's initial foxes were obtained from Soviet fox-fur farms (this origin has recently been questioned, but not the basic findings of the work [Gorman]).

As part of her work in the domestication experiment, Trut's made tameness observations. In it she would open the door of a fox's cage and then simply place a stick inside it. Given the aggressive nature of the foxes Trut wore 2 inch thick gloves for protection. Next, she would observe and record the response of the fox. During the early generations the responses she elicited were mostly akin to that of "fire breathing dragons: they were extremely aggressive when I approached or put the stick into the cage". Trut felt that these foxes "would have loved to rip my hand off." Additionally, there were also other foxes that would fearfully cower in the back of their cages. Both of these types of responses - aggressive and fearful - earned low tameness scores. Finally, there were a few foxes in the early days of the experiment that would calmly observe with little response. These calm foxes "were not especially prosocial towards people - they [simply] seemed to tolerate" them. Nonetheless, in the initial stages of the domestication experiment these were the foxes selected for mating in order to test the domestication hypothesis.

By the fourth and fifth generation some of the tameness-bred foxes, though, responded positively to humans. Some of these tiny pups "would wag their tales in anticipation" as Lyudmila Trut approached their cage. But the big breakthrough came with the sixth generation when as chronicled in a 2009 *Bioessays* paper, "there appeared pups that eagerly sought contacts with humans, not only [tail] wagging [but] also whining, whimpering, and licking in a dog-like manner." These remarkably transformed foxes were deemed the "elites" and they would even look up in response to their names. These elite foxes also opened their eyes a day earlier and responded to sounds a couple of days earlier than expected. Those premature developments left the authors wondering if the elites were in fact "preparing to start interacting with people as soon as possible." At the time the elites made up only 2% of the fox population, whereas now that figure is about 70%.

In order to investigate the presumed genetic basis behind the production of the tame or elite foxes, Siberian experimenters decided on some further procedures. One was to pursue a complementary subset of foxes that were bred for their aggressive attitude towards humans. The article characterized the resulting mean foxes as akin to the "multiheaded hound of Hades that guards the gates of the Underworld". In another procedure the experimenters decided to try switching some embryos from tame to mean mothers, and also vice versa. If the behavioral developments they had witnessed were really biologically-based - in particular caused by DNA specifications for tameness versus anti-tameness - then the resulting transplant-based kits should really stand out because of their behaviors. Conveniently, the coat color of a fox is determined genetically, and this allowed for the identification of a kit's biological parents. The embryo transplantation process was carried out about one week into the pregnancies of the expectant moms.

Trut and a colleague recorded the subsequent litters' responses to humans. With regards to one aggressive female mom it was reported that when her foster tame pups:

> were barely walking, ... if there was a human standing by they were already rushing to the cage doors and wagging their tails. This improper behavior appeared to vex the mother - she growled at the tame pups, grabbed their necks and threw them back in the nest.

Amongst that mom's genetic offspring, though, when they encountered a person:

> they growled aggressively and ran on their own to their nests. We saw this pattern repeatedly - pups behaved like their genetic mothers, not their surrogate mothers. Tameness and aggression towards humans thus appeared to be genetic traits.

This experimental finding is at minimum a remarkable confirmation of the existence of different innate behavioral tendencies. Unless there were critical contributions during the first week in utero (prior to switching the embryos), very little room was left for nurture's influence. So in this case the Nature-versus-Nurture debate appears settled.

From genetics' point of view this clearly indicates a DNA-basis for a very significant behavioral transformation. Furthermore, at the end of the article there is mention of preliminary identification of some of the DNA responsible for the changes in tameness, as well as the features of domestication syndrome. It is said to be located on chromosome number 12. Given the track record of such preliminary findings, though, it would be a good idea to take a wait-and-see stance. In any case, this ongoing experiment has been a landmark success for demonstrating some of the dynamics believed to be associated with behavioral genetics and also evolutionary genetics.

If future work could nail down the responsible DNA then this domestication would constitute an outstanding confirmation of evolutionary principles. It might also go a long way toward confirming the "secret of life" characterization of DNA. In fact several years ago I saw a review by Richard Dawkins of an intelligent design book in which Dawkins playfully used the presumed DNA basis for the domestication of canines in his rebuttal of the book.

There appear to be at least two problems facing this DNA-domestication genetic inference, though. The first is that if DNA is responsible for these changes then why have human behavioral genetics' searches failed thus far? If six selectively bred generations of foxes can produce a profound shift in innate aggressiveness, then why can't human studies identify specific DNA for aggressiveness? And why is the formidable schizophrenia genetics team failing in its efforts? If the genetics behind the transformation of foxes were to be identified that would put considerable pressure on human genome studies. Having human beings as exceptions to genetic principles would likely be unacceptable to geneticists, biologists, and scientists in general.

The second problem facing a genetic basis for the fox domestication experiment is one of plausibility. Is DNA really capable of producing such profound and apparently human-focused shifts in behavior? That is wagging, whining, whimpering, and licking in response to human contact in a dog-like fashion. The elites also responded to their names and the "acoustic dynamics of their vocalizations are remarkably similar to human laughter". Furthermore, there is the mysterious shift towards a human friendly appearance (which is consistent with the domestication syndrome). Such transformations genetically imply profound behavioral effects associated with DNA. How plausible is this given the inherent messiness of DNA and ultimately molecular-only nature of the underlying process? To use another expression that I saw Dawkins use - in this case in defense of materialism - do geneticists really believe in their "heart of hearts" that DNA can fully explain these domestication transformations?

Note that I am dodging another contrarian line of reasoning here. Others might accept the complete DNA basis for these transformations but claim that simple physics-only processes are very unlikely to have accomplished the requisite changes in DNA. While I tend to agree with the plausibility of this line of reasoning, I still stick with what I believe is the bigger pending question. That is, can DNA really do the job? Yes, in a few singular ways DNA specifics appear to be correlated with strong gross behavioral effects, as with Down syndrome. With the domestication of foxes, though, DNA would have to explain an amazing constellation of human-friendly changes.

Going a bit further here, the nature of the transformation from foxes to dogs implies profound genetic capabilities. Similarly, historically there was the subsequent binning of dogs into a variety of breeds. Across those breeds there are extraordinary differences including in their behavioral instincts. Is Watson correct in simply assuming that "[d]og shows are celebrations of the power of genes" and that as impressive as the morphological differences between breeds are, it is the behavioral differences that are "most impressive". I agree with Watson on the relative impressiveness of the innate behavioral differences, differences which span a Labrador retriever's "pliant and affectionate" nature; to the "twitchy"-ness of greyhounds; to the rounding-up instincts of a border collie; and onto pit bull's "canine embodiment of aggression" [Watson 2017, pp.386-387]. Additionally, there are such standout behaviors as found with the pointing in the pointer breeds. But is it realistic to believe that DNA's biochemical dynamics can encode, and specifically completely encode, for such innate behavioral differentiation?

This line of questioning will continue herein, in particular in the following chapter. I reflect back for a moment here, to the Preface's hyperthymesia, and question whether it is feasible for DNA to encode for a brain capable of such effortless and ongoing dated memories? Next, for an introductory prodigy sample I present a description of a musical one taken from Darold Treffert's fine *Islands of Genius*. The boy, Jay, by age 5 had composed five symphonies. The last of these was 190 pages (and 1328 bars) in length and ended up being performed by the London Symphony Orchestra and recorded by Sony Records. As described:

[o]n a *60 Minutes* program in 2006 Jay's parents stated that Jay spontaneously began to draw little cellos on paper at age two. Neither parent was particularly musically inclined, and there were never any musical instruments, including a cello, in the home. At age three Jay asked if he could have a cello of his own. The parents took him to a music store and to their astonishment Jay picked up a miniature cello and began to play it. He had never seen a real cello before that day. After that he began to draw miniature cellos and placed them on music lines. That was the beginning of his composing.

Jay says that the music just streams into his head at lightning speed, sometimes several symphonies running simultaneously. "My unconscious directs my conscious mind at a mile a minute," he told the correspondent on that program [Treffert, pp.55-56].

Treffert's book contains a number of examples supporting his conclusion that prodigal behavior typically involves "know[ing] things [that were] never learned". Such outcomes also represent remarkable transformations from the usual norms of childhood development (and the word "elite" from the fox study could well apply here in a musical sense). From a genetics perspective these transformations, like the canine domestication dynamics, require what appears to be incredible DNA contributions. As the late prominent biologist Ernst Mayr said, "[t]he entire behavioral information available to the newborn is contained in its DNA" [Mayr, p.253].

D. Some Additional Context and Two Possible Explanations

For more context on the significance of the missing heritability problem, you can look to Ernst Mayr's *What Evolution Is* which provides a finely written synopsis of science's understanding of the evolution of life [Mayr]. Mayr's synopsis highlights two scientific assumptions about evolution. The first is that evolutionary processes simply reflect physics-dictated phenomena, with no underlying direction. Molecules just doing their thing. Mayr offers a little defense of this physics-only assumption, whilst as earlier mentioned, others have questioned it. The second assumption is that DNA is capable of fulfilling its life/evolutionary roles and Mayr doesn't even acknowledge this assumption. As science sees it all of life must be material-only and consistent with physics. This confidence in materialism-only evolution is captured nicely in Mayr's book, beginning with its title.

That complete confidence in DNA's functioning is also reflected in Siddartha Mukherjee's 2016 book, *The Gene,* and moreover echoed in its reception. Mukherjee's book clearly captured the materialism of genetics. The book was highly praised and as far as I could see the logic of genetics was never questioned. It is also of note that Mukherjee made a point of predicting success for the genomic searches by "the end of the decade". As of this writing in 2019 is that prediction looking accurate? A look at the early 2019 Amazon reviews for *The Gene* reveals almost all 5 star reviews, with one 3 star review protesting the lack of political correctness in a politically correct-bent book! One of the 5 star reviews nicely captured the common tendency towards science-awed rapture, "[a] Majestic and brilliant work, beautifully written, and informative, and evocative". Similarly, is James D. Watson's analogous "extremely hopeful" take on genetics and mental illnesses panning out? As of this writing I have seen nothing consistent with meaningful success in either behavioral genetics or personal genomics research.

At this point I think that it looks quite likely that the expectations of behavioral genetics and personal genomics will fail. If the missing heritability situation constituted an "absolutely beyond belief" failure in 2008, then it has to be a notch up in 2019. Furthermore, the unsuccessful status of the genetic searches implicitly argues for plenty of non-functional content among the variable portions of our genomes. If you compare the outcomes of many individuals differing in one or more variable DNA-lettering and find no corresponding differences in their outcomes, then that suggests those variable letters could well have little functional significance. This appears inline with existing claims about the prevalence of junk (or neutral) DNA. One evolutionary biologist, T. Ryan Gregory, has claimed that given the haphazard dynamics of evolution that "only 8 percent, plus or minus 1 percent" of human DNA is likely to be functional [Zimmer]. In fact the unfolding heritability deficit suggests that the 8 percent figure might be generous.

On this point it is worth noting that intelligent design work (see for example *Darwin's Doubt* by Stephen C. Meyer) seems to imply that there is only a little junk DNA. This may makes sense from the perspective of an intelligent designer but with the additional evidence that even the variable DNA contains plenty of non-functional or junk elements, that design hypothesis appears to get be undermined.

So if the origins of our individual behavioral inclinations turn out to be independent of our DNA, then how much confidence should we have in a genetic basis for the species- or gender-specific behavioral tendencies that are presumed by evolutionary psychology? Differences in innate behavioral aspects are supposed to have their roots in DNA differences, whether they happen to occur between two same-sex individuals or more broadly across the standard equipment of different genders and/or species.

Moving on here it is worth considering two possible alternative explanations for the missing heritability. One explanation was given in a 2010 article that was previously quoted. That was the very interesting and significant "The Great DNA Deficit: Are Genes for Disease a Mirage" article by Jonathan Latham and Allison Wilson of Ithaca, New York's Bioscience Resource Project. In that article they lay out what they feel is a very strong case against the existence of the DNA origins expected in personal genomics.

Their claim is that the origins of complex disease occurrences are simply environmental and that the apparent heredity reflects faulty studies involving the relative outcomes of monozygotic (identical) twin pairs and dizygotic (fraternal) twin pairs. They build their environmental argument by first looking at accepted environmental causes. They point out that "[p]eople who migrate acquire the spectrum of diseases of their adopted country". Their citation here is to the results described in *The China Study* (2004) by Cornell University's T. Colin Campbell along with his son, Thomas M. Campbell II [Campbell]. That study appears to demonstrate strong statistical correlations between our diet and the likelihood of our encountering common complex diseases, including cancer and heart disease (the strength of the study is that up until not too long ago many people in China lived local lives and consumed the corresponding local/traditional diets, and ultimately exhibited disease occurrence rates differing by location). The resulting recommendation is to move towards a whole foods, plant-based diet. The overlapping Ithaca origins of that popular study and the Bioscience Resource Project probably accounts for some of Latham and Wilson's commitment to, and enthusiasm for, an environmental explanation.

As it turns out I am a fan of *The China Study* and also vegan, but I don't accept Latham and Wilson's reasoning here. The recommended plant-based diet may be helpful health-(and also sustainability-)wise, but that does not preclude the possibility of significant innate factors at work here as well.

Such factors could then differentiate the outcomes of individuals who happen to eat similar diets and also have similar environmental exposures. Such innate factors are scientifically supposed to have DNA origins (as they do for certain particular genetic conditions). Geneticists have been doing disease-related twin studies for a long time now and they have consistently demonstrated that monozygotic twins pairs are more consistent in their disease experiences than are fraternal twin pairs across a number of disease conditions. Such studies suggest for example that about 80 percent of the cause of the occurrence of the mental illness schizophrenia is genetic [Balter] and the remaining 20 percent is environmental. That high estimate reflects the fact of a roughly 50 percent concurrence rate amongst monozygotic twin pairs versus only about 10 percent amongst dizygotic (or fraternal) pairs. Thus, if you are a monozygotic twin and your twin sibling experiences schizophrenia then it is appears to be about 50 percent likely that you also will.

There certainly are very significant environmental connections to diseases as for example found with smoking and lung cancer. But there also is long established evidence of differing innate susceptibility factors across a number of diseases for individuals and also as grossly evident with the patterns of disease occurrences among families. Do Wilson and Latham think that the susceptibility to schizophrenia and autism is based on diet and/or other environmental factors? Additionally, beyond experiencing trauma, can they suggest environmental factors contributing to either of these conditions? The occurrence rates for schizophrenia appear to be "about 1 percent throughout the world, notwithstanding vast environmental and socioeconomic differences across societies" [Balter]. Latham and Wilson bring in some arguments from the earlier Nature versus Nurture academic battles, arguments in particular that appear to write off twin studies due to purportedly flawed environmental assumptions and even going so far as to cite an academic's claim that "human heritability ... [is] a 'poisonous concept'". From my own personal observations I think that the straightforward logic used to estimate heritability using twins makes sense.

Instead of going into elaborate arguments with regards to environmental versus innate contributions, I think it is probably better to walk away from the somewhat subtle disease susceptibility realm (can you look at person you meet and sense such susceptibilities?). Looking in the behavioral inclination arena, on the other hand, offers much clearer evidence for variable aspect of innate characteristics. Is any non-academic-affiliated adult willing to argue that there aren't clear differences in personalities and also in gross behavioral phenomena like intelligence? This should be readily apparent to anyone who grew up with siblings. These differences show up early and appear to be rather deeply etched which is supposed to imply a genetic connection. Notice also that even if these tendencies were caused by spontaneous mutations (as opposed to passed along directly from parents), then some of those genetic details should still show up in genome searches. Furthermore, for those wanting a vivid sample of the variations in human intelligence, let me suggest doing some volunteer tutoring. Analogous to sports you will likely encounter some big differences in abilities. There may be other forms of intelligence as some have argued, but there certainly is evident a conceptual learning attribute termed "intelligence" and, for better and not better, it is quite significant in the modern world.

Latham and Wilson even go further down a questionable track in that they bring politicians and corporations into their explanation. Both of these entities are claimed to "like genetic determinism" because it potentially shifts blame for ill-health in the public away from them. I will return later to critically consider such liberal or academic perspectives.

Continuing here with a second possible heredity explanation, I turn to Rupert Sheldrake's extension of existing ideas involving morphogenetic fields. Sheldrake builds on earlier efforts which argued against the plausibility of DNA being able to fully specify our innate details. In particular, how is it that DNA - which codes for the linear layout of amino acids comprising proteins - can ultimately specify our very complicated forms? In addition to the big coverage in his book, *The Presence of the Past* [Sheldrake 2012a], Sheldrake also offers more succinct descriptions including a one page synopsis [Sheldrake bet]. That page is paired with the biologist Lewis Wolpert's contrary synopsis and together they form a modest bet. In Sheldrake's one page statement he begins with a sort of bottom-up argument against plausibility of genetics:

> [g]enes code for the linear sequences of amino acids in proteins, which then fold up into complex three-dimensional forms. Wolpert's wager presupposes that the folding of proteins can be computed from first principles, given the sequence of amino acids specified by the genes. So far, this has proven impossible. As in all bottom-up calculations, there is a combinatorial explosion. For example, by random folding, the amino acid chain of the enzyme ribonuclease, a small protein, could adopt more than 10^{40}

different shapes, which could take billions of years to explore. In fact, it folds into its habitual form in 2 minutes.

The folding of proteins does appear to be a serious complexity challenge, but I think that it is likely that some of the claimed 10^{40} different shapes are not possible. A linear sequence can not be folded in such a way as to produce overlapping positioning of different molecules. Additionally, Sheldrake furthers his implausibility case by suggesting that the complexity challenges for establishing the structure of cells are even worse. He goes on to introduce the hypothesized approach based on fields:

> [r]andom molecular permutations simply cannot explain how organisms work. Instead, cells, tissues and organs develop in a modular manner, shaped by morphogenetic fields, first recognized [or hypothesized] by developmental biologists in the 1920s.

The idea here is that physical fields somehow channel the developing embryo towards an endpoint of an individual organism's physical form (and also more subtly, the corresponding behavioral patterns). Thus DNA is claimed to simply provide molecular recipes for the body's proteins, whilst morphogenetic fields are claimed to shape those ingredients into functioning organisms.

Rupert Sheldrake appears convinced that the original ideas involving fields are roughly accurate. A significant contribution of his appears to be hypothesizing that such fields are a memory-bearing aspect of reality. His hypothesis suggests that:

> developing organisms are tuned to similar past organisms, which act as morphic "transmitters". Their tuning depends on the presence of appropriate genes and proteins, and genetic inheritance helps explain why they are tuned in to morphic fields of their own species: a frog's egg tunes in to frog fields rather than newt or goldfish fields because it is already a frog cell containing frog genes and proteins [Sheldrake 2012a, p.155].

And thus "the forms of the cells, tissues, organs, and the organisms as a whole are shaped not by DNA but by morphic fields" [p.154]. Furthermore, he suggests that the:

> inherited behavior of animals is likewise organized by morphic fields. Genetic changes can affect both the form and behavior, but these patterns of activity are inherited by morphic resonance [p.154].

In a very broad way Sheldrake feels that a number of mysteries in life - beginning with inheritance - imply the existence of a series of these shaping or guiding fields.

I find Sheldrake's works to be very interesting, although they can sometimes be a bit tough to read because of their formal and philosophical style. He does, though, include a significant point with regards to the existing limits of proposed intelligent design-based claims. In *The Presence of the Past* he points out that such theories really don't challenge materialism (and with it determinism), there would just be some external intelligent input into the ongoing evolutionary process. In the end, though, it would still be molecules acting like molecules that would define life as we know it. I agree about the lack of significance of such design proposals. But how does the introduction of a whole bunch of information or morphic fields change life, or more particularly, who/what we are? It appears to be just more physics along with the ingredients list and in the end life can still be defined via physical processes (now admittedly more complicated), resulting in the same basic implications that entities like self are just artifacts (or emergent phenomena) derived from physics.

This contradiction is significant in that Sheldrake's work appears to be motivated not just to challenge the existing scientific vision, but also support a deeper vision of life. For example he writes, "[t]he Father is the source of the formative principle" [p.357] and "[f]rom the very beginning, the universe has been inflated as if by a creative breath blowing it up" [p.357]. He has also written 3 books on spirituality - *Science and Spiritual Practices: Transformative Experiences and Their Effects on Our Bodies, Brains, and Health*; *Ways to Go Beyond and Why They Work: Spiritual Practices in a Scientific Age*; and *The Physics of Angels: Exploring the Realm Where Science and Spirit Meet*. But if morphic fields are simply physical fields then I don't see this as really changing the gist of the materialist model.

On the other hand, given the unfolding crisis confronting the genetics, Sheldrake should not be shunned or ridiculed by biologists. His heresy is not serious as any form of dualism would be, it simply appears to entail more elaborate physics (including the presence of memory within the morphic fields). Continuing, in *The Presence of the Past* Sheldrake seems to claim that these morphic (or formative causation) ideas could also be extended into useful explanations of our "evolving" universe. He also refers to "evolutionary cosmology" as though it were an established entity. I have not been able to find any references consistent with these evolutionary ideas, though. He may have just gone overboard in his efforts to generalize the morphic concept.

I also found that Sheldrake's heredity explanation appears anchored in an inaccuracy. He goes to considerable lengths to suggest that the incredible similarities noted amongst monozygotic twins, in particular those who were raised separately, could not simply be the result of genes alone. He wrote:

> morphic resonance between [monozygotic twins] will be exceptionally specific and stronger than that between any other pairs of humans. As a result, patterns of activity, beliefs, habits, or health patterns in one are likely to influence the other. Therefore, many of the remarkable similarities between identical twins may depend on morphic resonance rather than genes [p.180].

The idea here is that physical fields are likely required to explain some of the amazing similarities such as when two separated shortly after birth twins were both found to live in "the only house on the block, with a white bench around a back tree in the backyard; both were interested in stock car racing; both had elaborate workshops where they made miniature picnic tables or miniature rocking chairs" [p.180].

Steven Pinker similarly pointed out that despite gross differences in environmental exposures:

> [i]dentical twins separated at birth share traits like entering the water backwards and only up to their knees, sitting out elections because they feel insufficiently informed, obsessively counting everything in sight, becoming captain of the volunteer fire department, and leaving little love notes around the house for their wives [Pinker 1997, p.20].

An earlier mentioned alternative explanation, though, was provided by the biologist James D. Watson. In it such shared behaviors are viewed as most likely simply coincidences [Watson 2017, pp.378-379]. Watson offered an example in that he and his two (unrelated) coauthors have all owned Volvo station wagons.

The point missing here, though, is that the prime mystery posed by monozygotic twins is not their similarities, but the scale of their differences. The fact that their appearances are typically so similar makes genetic sense (conceivably furthered by something akin to morphogenetic resonance). The fact that they are so wholesale different in a behavioral sense does not, and thus the same Steven Pinker can acknowledge that "something is happening here but we don't know what it is" [Pinker 2002, p.380]. This mystery is well established in psychology (and should have tempered Pinker's endorsement of genetic determinism) and moreover is readily apparent in person. In an effort to try to address this mystery the researcher Judith R. Harris wrote the book *No Two Alike* [Harris J. R.]. That book opens with one identical twin telling a reporter that she and her twin "have different world views, we have different lifestyles, we think very differently about issues" [Harris J. R., p.1]. That twin also added "[w]e are two completely separate individuals who are stuck to each other". Those twins were conjoined and sadly died as a result of their separation surgery. Such differences are perhaps not surprising given the differences observable between other monozygotic twins, whether they were raised together or apart. How this can happen given the assumptions of genetics is a real mystery. How this can happen when morphic fields are supposed to make them even more similar should be puzzling Rupert Sheldrake.

Furthermore, if we are to take environmental explanations seriously, like those suggested by Latham and Wilson, then how can such differences show up amongst monozygotic twins regardless of whether they grew up together or not? The surprisingly large health differences observed between monozygotic twins were described in a 2006 *New York Times* article by Gina Kolata [Kolata]. Kolata's article opened by describing a healthy and active 92 year old and her monozygotic twin. Both had grown up together and went on to live in the same area. The other twin, though, had experienced incontinence; had had a hip replaced; experienced a "degenerative disorder that destroyed most of her vision"; and also had dementia. Describing these large differences was an appropriate warmup to the rest of the article which communicated the very surprising differences observed in a large study on twin longevity. Monozygotic twins' longevities were only marginally closer than those of fraternal twins, and the former were found to die on average "more than 10 years apart". This led one of the study's authors to comment that "how tall your parents are compared to the average height explains 80 to 90 percent of how tall you are compared to the average person [but] only 3 percent of how long you live compared to the average person can be explained by how long your parents lived". Results such as this should have moderated genomic expectations as well as support for environmental-based theories. Puzzling results like these should receive a lot more media coverage.

I close off this look at alternative explanations for the missing heritability by noting that unusual but accepted behavioral phenomena also provide hurdles for such explanations. Such phenomena will be considered in the next chapter and they are certainly difficult to square with any plausible DNA functioning or realistic environmental and/or morphogenetic contributions too.

E. A Little Perspective from Physics and Psychiatry

An interesting comparison can be found in physics' really big topic of dark matter. From careful astronomical observations it is apparent to physicists/astronomers that the visible matter of the universe provides an inadequate basis for the large scale motion of the universe. Somehow there have to be some additional forces at play. There appear to be two kinds of these forces. One are attractive or gravity-like forces and these are presumed to arise from non-visible stuff termed "dark matter". Somehow then this invisible dark matter produces gravity forces that are believed to be responsible for the additional attractive forces apparent in the motions inside galaxies. The other mysterious force is believed to be responsible for the accelerating expansion of the universe and it is termed "dark energy". This is commonly hypothesized to be a property of space and it is somehow causing the accelerating spread between galaxies. Together these two, in a gravity sense for dark matter and in an energy-based sense for dark energy, are thought to compromise the equivalent of about 95% of the mass-energy of the universe. Thus "normal" matter - the stuff we can directly observe and traditional physics has examined - constitutes a small minority of the universe (and as such "normal" is perhaps inappropriate).

In the case of the dark matter mystery, there has been a rather large research effort underway for three decades now to detect signs of the existence of the hypothesized dark particles. In particular researchers have been searching for subtle signs of interaction between dark matter particles and regular matter. In an August 2018 *Scientific American* article, "Is Dark Matter Real?", by Sabin Hossenfelder and Stacy S. McGaugh [Hossenfelder and McGaugh] these efforts were described as experiments that:

place large tanks of liquified noble gases or carefully prepared solids, kept at extremely low temperatures, in well-shielded environments such as underground mines to avoid contamination from cosmic radiation. Sensitive detectors patiently wait for telltale signs of a dark matter particle bouncing off an atomic nucleus in the liquid or solid target.

Hossenfelder and McGaugh then go on to point out that none of these searches has uncovered evidence for dark particles. Additionally, the authors point out some challenges for any explanation involving dark matter. Conceptually while such invisible particles could provide some of the missing gravity required to explain the motion within galaxies, they appear challenged in trying to explain some more subtle aspects of observed galactic dynamics.

Hossenfelder and McGaugh then went on to discuss a potential alternative take on the mystery. That alternative is that what astronomers are seeing is in fact the result of some novel aspects of the force of gravity. They refer to these potential explanatory routes as "modified gravity" theories. This is inherently a bit heretical as the approach questions the completeness of Einstein's theory of general relativity. It also does not require additional particles. The authors do what appears to be a good job of providing some balanced arguments, for and against, this alternative explanation involving a modified form of gravity.

What is of significance here with regards to the missing heritability situation is that in the missing dark matter situation, physicists have a plan B to fall back on. Although the pursuit of plan B runs into significant inertia - for reasons including the requisite challenging of Einstein and also the novel particle-hypothesizing inclinations of theoretical physicists - researchers can look elsewhere and apparently keep their jobs and even get an article in *Scientific American*. Hossenfelder and McGaugh point out in their article that currently "a few dozen of scientists are studying modified gravity, whereas several thousand are looking for particle dark matter". The plan B research effort then might be chugging along in modest fashion.

Before plunging back into the genetics scenario I add a bit more from physics-land. In the dark matter research world there are even more approaches to consider. The dark matter-questioning authors also went on to point out a possible plan C in which "the truth is in between [A and B]: a type of dark matter that can masquerade as modified gravity". In what I would suggest is the over-hyped realm of physics, researchers are given plenty of freedom to speculate (more like SPECULATE) in pursuit of explanations. This can be inferred by looking at established theories about possible quantum realities and also from speculations about possible parallel universes.

Now back to heritability where there really is very little analogous freedom for geneticists. I suggest that biologists/geneticists are effectively in the front lines of the defense of materialism. That foundational scientific belief that life is completely describable in terms of physics dictates that DNA fulfill the heredity role. Never mind some of the extraordinary behavioral challenges, DNA has to cover all of materialism's bets. For a sense of the situation a couple of quotes by James D. Watson will do:

> I was born curious. ... And so if you wanted an explanation for life, it had to be about the molecular basis for life. I never thought there was a spiritual basis for life; I was very lucky to be brought up by a father who had no religious beliefs [Watson 2003].

And in commenting on a promotional line used for the (genetics-inspired) movie *Gattaca* - "There is no gene for the human spirit" - Watson wrote, "[i]t remains a dangerous blind spot in our society that so many wish this were so" [Watson 2017, p.440]. Readers might keep Watson's scientific perspective and his own potential blind spot in mind as they consider some unusual behavioral challenges in the next chapter.

There is one conceivable alternative materialist basis for some heredity, though, and that is epigenetic contributions. Epigenetics involves information stored not directly in the DNA letter sequence but in the form of the physical packaging of the long string-like DNA molecule. The established aspects of epigenetic functioning consist of allowing for the specialization of cells for different tissues, and also in some apparent contributions towards the conditioning of the brain. That same process might then be considered another possible route for inheritance. But it appears that even epigenetic researchers are very modest in their expectations in this regard. The particular area in which experimental evidence has been suggestive of extra-genetic contributions to heredity, is with regards to psychological trauma [Carey]. In one overview of possible epigenetic heredity contributions, the researcher Eric Nestler pointed out that "[o]f course we now know that an individual's genes play the dominant [heredity] role in determining physiology and function" [Nestler]. Nestler went on in a followup conversation to state that any epigenetic inheritance effect is "controversial" [Nestler podcast].

That controversy reflects the apparent obstacles to any inheritance via an epigenetic mechanism. Those obstacles are formidable and thus many geneticists completely reject that possibility [Carey]. Consistent with this James Watson described those epigenetic-heredity hurdles [Watson 2017, p.384]. In brief, the molecules contributing to the epigenetic-packaging (or shaping) of the genome are believed to be stripped off twice before forming egg or sperm cells. As Watson put it, "the DNA that goes into the eggs and sperm are stripped clean of epigenetic marks [or molecules], resulting in the fertilized egg being the epigenetic equivalent of a blank slate". One possible opening for epigenetic contributions to inheritance, though, was pointed out by the epigenetic epidemiologist, Karin Michels, in an article in *Harvard Magazine*. Michels suggested that could happen:

> through a distinct and poorly understood mechanism called genomic imprinting. This transgenerational inheritance seems to be limited to genes that control growth during fetal development [Shaw 2017].

In that nice succinct article, Michels also made clear how difficult it is to weed out possible effects in offspring that were truly inherited (including from epigenetic sources) from those based on environmental exposures in the womb. This difficulty she believes casts a significant doubt on a number of the claims involving epigenetic inheritance. In conclusion it appears that there could be a small window for some epigenetic inheritance. A related mystery would seem to be how such epigenetic marks would then migrate through the developmental stages, and on to their previous cell type where they could then echo the effects found in their parents (in some type of brain cell likely for behavioral tendencies).

For some personal perspectives on the genetics relevant landscape, you can read Andrew Solomon's engaging big book about unusual children and their families, *Far From the Tree* [Solomon]. When reading Solomon's book it is easy to be impressed with the mysteries some of the children represent. It is also very easy to be moved by the big challenges those children represent and by the corresponding remarkable commitments they elicit from some parents. Solomon does not have a scientist's background so his discussions about these kids and their families tends to range somewhat far and wide (including perhaps too much psychoanalytical speculation - how well can we really even know our own motivations?). As expected possible genetic explanations regularly show up in *Far From the Tree*. In addition to conditions involving previously identified mutations like Down's Syndrome (involving the presence of an extra copy of chromosome 21), the remaining unusual innate conditions or tendencies considered in Solomon's book are also expected to have their own genetic origins. In his chapter on kids who grew up to commit crimes and seemed to be criminally inclined, Solomon wrote that:

> [a]rguments about the nature-or-nurture origin of criminality are just as engaged as those about the origin of autism or genius. The National Institutes of Health's Maribeth Champoux and her colleagues have shown that newborn monkeys with a gene for extreme aggression will not grow up to be aggressive if they are cross-fostered to extremely gentle mothers, even though the aggression gene is still biologically active in them. In human beings, criminal behavior has been related to a genetic irregularity associated with changed function in a particular serotonin transporter [Solomon, p.563].

Solomon went on to point out that in humans, "the [aggression] gene appears to confer not criminal behavior, but a vulnerability to develop such behavior under certain circumstances" [Solomon, p.564]. Here we see a belief in a genetic contribution as well as the very common tendency to soften possible genetic determinism.

What is of significance here is that these confident discussions published in 2012 are now forgotten. Like many other genetic findings they were perhaps marginal at the time and since then have been negated. Readers can look up discussions in a book like Pinker's *Better Angels of Our Nature* for some established rebuttals to such aggression gene findings (but naturally paired with arguments ultimately supporting a genetic basis) [Pinker 2011, pp.611-622]. In this way the missing heritability problem is perhaps most tangible as the missing headline problem. If science truly had a solid handle on an aggression gene(s) it would have been huge news. In a publication like the *New York Times* it would have produced a very big front page headlines and stories. Furthermore the *Times* would have certainly had additional articles to allay fears about genetic determinism, perhaps in the form of pieces describing notable positive people that had the dreaded aggression-promoting gene(s). The *Times* could well then have also played this development out in a political fashion by arguing that a progressive or

Democratic upbringing is more likely to minimize the ill effects of the gene contributing to aggression. Similarly significant findings of other DNA connections would have certainly produced large media followup.

Some of the possible significance of genetic reasoning is also found in *Far From the Tree*. In a chapter on raising children who were conceived of via rape, Solomon presented a number of poignant examples. In one of those some genetic reasoning showed up in a mom's quote:

> [h]alf of her genes are evil ... I can do whatever I should as her mom to make her this loving, wonderful, caring person. But in her is the DNA of a person who is really sick, and is that DNA stronger than what I can do? [Solomon, p.484].

Such genetic reasoning is natural fallout from the modern understanding of life, in effect a vision which Sam Harris characterized as being consistent with biochemical puppets. Further significance of genetic logic can be found in the enormous financial and intellectual commitment to uncovering the expected DNA origins. There is a lot more on the line with the missing heritability problem than there is with physics' dark mysteries.

Additionally, it turns out that traditional approaches to episodes of schizophrenia seem to have worked better than those based on the scientific vision. As Tanye Marie Luhrmann pointed out in her article "Beyond the Brain", "[s]chizophrenia has a more benign course and outcome in the developing world" [Luhrmann]. Luhrmann also touched an the underlying downside associated with science's bio-robotic perspective (a perspective nicely captured in the title, "Faulty Circuits", of an April 2010 *Scientific American* article by the director of the National Institute of Mental Health, Thomas Insel). In our country people with schizophrenia commonly spend a lot of time homeless in part because "[t]hey dislike the diagnosis even more than the idea of being out on the street, because for them the idea of being 'crazy'" is worse. Luhrmann also wrote that "Indian families don't treat people with schizophrenia as if they have a soul-destroying illness."

F. What About Philosophy?

For more perspective on the missing heritability problem as well as the influence of scientism, I now turn to the field of philosophy. For number of years now I have regularly visited Rochester, New York's Central (or downtown) library. Some of the library's departments provide tables or shelves displaying new books. One of my regular stops has been at the new religion and philosophy books' shelf. I have a general interest in this area so I have made a point of inspecting new releases.

Those stops are usually a disappointment, though, as I rarely encounter anything serious from either the religious or philosophy authors. For the most part the recent popular religious books tend to contain new presentations of faith-based reasoning, whilst the academic ones tend to be esoteric intellectual takes on ancient works. The new philosophy books on the other hand appear to partake in a different kind of faith, a faith that determined intellectually-styled inquiries into philosophical topics amounts to something important. For the most part, these philosophical works seem to embody a critical take I have encountered in reading and that is that philosophy is heavily invested in obscurantism. That is in trying to look smart through elaborate, difficult to follow arguments, or perhaps more simply with what might be termed serious bullshitting. This trend has been pointed out over the last decade or so by commenters with regards to the *New York Times'* philosophy column, The Stone.

Before moving on it is worth mentioning that neither of these new book genres has contained anything that appears to really challenge scientific materialism, which I suggests provides the foundation for scientism and also effectively eliminates any dualistic understanding of life. Even the big controversial book, *Mind and Cosmos,* by Thomas Nagel is simply another philosophical take on the so-called hard problem of consciousness. Consciousness or subjectivity is thus argued as demanding something more than contemporary physics's understanding for its explanation. Nagel clearly states his lack of questioning the objective accuracy of science's materialist vision [Nagel NYT]. Additionally, Nagel follows through with his suggested hard problem and claims it implies that the evolution of life - which beget the philosophically problematic subjectivity - required some additional input too. He not surprisingly favors a "naturalistic, though non-materialist, alternative" instead of a divinity-oriented explanation. Nagel's gist appears to be that physics needs to be updated to provide what might be termed a Materialist II explanation. Perhaps then, there is another subtle esoteric particle or two that needs to be hypothesized and then detected in order to advance a more physically and philosophically sound description of consciousness. But does Nagel's argument effectively challenge the deterministic or mechanistic implications of the materialist model? I suggest that it basically just adds a philosophical asterisk to the phenomena of consciousness.

Now I turn to my experiences in publishing papers. In the summer of 2017 I got a paper entitled "Science's Big Problem, Reincarnation's Big Potential, and Buddhists' Profound Embarrassment" published at an online academic journal *Religions* (this article is sort of a succinct introduction to the terrain of the book *A Hole in Science*) [Christopher 2017b]. This paper was published in a special issue on reincarnation and it drew a bit of attention. Somehow I had managed to get a paper questioning materialism and pointing out some possible reincarnation-based explanations (as well as critiquing the superficial intellectual makeovers currently afflicting Buddhism) out and into an academic-affiliated journal.

Other outsiders may well have tried to get their own heretical manuscripts published and been stymied along the way. As a sample of the difficulty facing outsider manuscripts, my efforts to get my pending *Religions* paper published at an associated preprint site immediately hit a standoff. Some science-trained individuals at that site quickly refused to publish the paper until it had been assessed for credibility. After a week, though, they got back and acknowledged it was ok for preprint publication.

On a sober point, though, even this nominal success ultimately confirmed my skepticism about academics. Not a single academic contacted me afterwords on what was a unique paper. Given the significance of some of the arguments made, I think this is a testimony to the inability of academics to question science. On the positive side, the publishing crew at mdpi.com were very helpful. But my experiences with philosophy have been even more sobering. For over ten years, now, I have been sending simple 'Hey I think there are some simple challenges to materialism as well as a big heritability crisis unfolding, perhaps you might find this interesting. Sincerely, Ted Christopher'-notes to philosophers. These have elicited essentially zero response. Well, maybe they have better things to contemplate.

In the summer of 2018 I decided to take the heritability crisis further and introduce some possible evolutionary implications. A philosophy journal/website (Open Journal of Philosophy - OJPP) had contacted me about a coming Philosophy of Religion issue so I decided to put together a manuscript entitled "The Heritability Challenge to Evolution and Materialism: An Opening for Religious Perspectives" and submit it. This was accepted. After it got published I quickly realized something was wrong. First, there turned out to be no other religion-relevant papers [Christopher 2018]. The *OJPP* people informed me that there were insufficient manuscripts submitted to produce a Philosophy of Religions issue. In fact from what I could see of the papers published around the time of my (on-time) paper there were no other papers addressing a religious perspective. Perhaps more fallout from the clout of science.

But the real news was seeing the subsequent downloading statistics for the set of papers published around the same time (roughly August 2018). My paper was seeing very little action. That is, a paper with the succinct abstract:

> There are under-appreciated, serious behavioral challenges to science's understanding of life and its evolution. The general challenge to that understanding, though, has unfolded in the form of pervasive failures in the search for the DNA origins of many heritable characteristics. Science has placed enormous faith in the presumed workings of DNA, including of course as a foundation for evolution. The stunning inability to identify the DNA bases for many heritable characteristics amongst humans - sometimes termed the missing heritability problem - is a big challenge to the largely unquestioned, biological vision. This situation is discussed herein along with its possible implications for religious perspectives.

drew very little attention. Perhaps then the concurrent philosophical submissions were hitting more significant topics and thus drawing greater interest.

I introduce some of the competing content via an example of the material that drew significant interest. A prominent draw was to a paper entitled, "Processes of Science and Art Modeled as a Holoflux of Information Using Toroidal Geometry" and its (long) abstract began:

> An attempt is made to model the structure of science and art discovery processes in the light of currently defined ideas on the societal flow of knowledge and conservation of information, using the versatile physical concept of toroidal geometry. This should be seen as a heuristic model that is open for further development and evolution. The scientific process, has been often described as a[n] iterative and/or recurrent process. Current models explain the generation of new knowledge on the basis of a number of sequential steps (activities) operating in circular mode. This model intrinsically assumes this process to be congruent for all individual scientific efforts. Yet, such a model is obviously inadequate to fully describe the whole integral process of scientific discovery as an ongoing interactive process, performed in a cumulative fashion. This implies that any new cycle

> starts from a different perspective or, optimistically seen, is initiated from a higher level, in a spiral mode that takes into account the ongoing rise of scientific perspectives. Also, any model that attempts to picture the scientific process, should include potential interactions of concepts or hypotheses, in the sense that concurrently developed concepts may (mutually) influence each other and may even be mixed or superimposed or, alternatively, may even result in concept extinction.

Then further along in this abstract:

> The dynamics of cognition and perception are fruitfully suggested by the rotational dynamics of a torus as a basis for its "self-reflexive" property. Also, the torus exhibits contraction/relaxation loops, in which the torus turns inside out in a vibrating mode, implying strange loop trajectories. This suggests that the toroidal geometry embodies a cognitive twist, relating the "inside" to "outside" of knowledge as a Mobius strip, a phenomenon that can be seen as the basis of personal experience, intuitive vision, intention, imagination, and technical realization of the becoming piece of art. The finalization of the art concept can be conceived as a sort of knotting of the spiral information process: [b]y literally connecting both ends of the toroidal information trajectory, the spiral is closed and a final product is created.

And finally for general perspective the abstract concluded with:

> Unfortunately, science that often claims objectivity, sometimes seems dominated by a range of subjective human attitudes, not different from any other field of society. One factor is the deficient science-philosophical education of our students in current curricula and the loss of academic worldview in university careers, in which "time is short" and necessary moments of reflection scarce.

This work appears to be highly speculative as well as abstract, and moreover it appears to be of little utility to anyone other than philosophers. If you could find people who sincerely would like to obtain a model of the discovery processes in science and art, I doubt they would want anything so abstract beginning with the questionable usage of the donut-like toroidal geometry. The processes of these kinds of discoveries are to put it simply, messy. An exception, though, might be the straightforward logic followed in some physics or astronomy efforts - wait for a new instrument and see what it reveals. What kind of helpful models of discovery really seem possible?

The biggest subjective blinder in contemporary science has to be materialism (or physicalism) and that limitation is in fact shared by contemporary philosophy (which I think has pushed philosophy into a serious rut). Furthermore, what would be the potential benefits to science in picking up on philosophy's materialist and verbose worldview?

I close this chapter by suggesting that if an analogous impasse were encountered by an alternative and/or religious understanding of life it would have certainly drawn attention. In fact, such an unfolding failure could well have become a source of humor, at least among the more strident followers of scientism. On the other hand, when the scientific understanding of life gets derailed in a big way it draws almost no interest. Even among the big thinkers of academia - in particular those living in the shadows of scientific materialism in fields like philosophy and religion - amazingly nobody appears willing to question genetics. I would be surprised if there wasn't a significant ongoing academic focus on the implications of genetic determinism.

CHAPTER 2 - HOW COULD SCIENCE HAVE OVERLOOKED THIS?

This essay wades into some astounding behavioral phenomena neglected by science. The essay will first consider some accepted but unusual behaviors. Then the coverage will shift to some taboo or paranormal phenomena.

Readers can keep in mind that per dictates of science the reports of taboo activity have to reflect some kind of combination of naivety and/or dishonesty; and more generally, all real behavioral phenomena must make molecular-only (or "jigglings and wigglings of atoms") sense in order to be consistent with the laws of physics. Additionally, all innate behavioral tendencies of course should have an underlying DNA basis, which in turn should be consistent with the workings of evolution.

A. Unusual but Accepted Phenomena - Prodigies

I get started here with some accepted behavioral challenges to materialism. In particular I consider exceptional intellectual predispositions and surprising gender orientations. In my earlier book I considered a number of intellectual mysteries including the Einstein Syndrome, prodigies, savants, and the Flynn Effect.

Included in that coverage was the previously mentioned case of a young boy who apparently had remarkable innate inclinations and skills with regards to playing a cello and also composing music. Such a case appears to capture a basic characteristic of prodigies in that they seem to show up in a relatively adult-focused fashion and this clearly challenges the scientific model. In Darold Treffert's *Islands of Genius* he characterizes this aspect by stating that savants appear to "indeed know things [and exhibit skills] that they never learned" [Treffert, p.59].

As a little preliminary background to this topic it is worth noting that our species in its evolutionary history branched off from chimpanzees. In so doing we left behind living largely in trees, and moved on to spread out across Africa and then elsewhere. This complicated trek involved interactions with other non-surviving hominids and also of course the development of our large brains. The latter development is believed to have come in significant part in response to increases in our social activity. But what particular scenario shaped the evolutionary specialization of our psyches? Steven Pinker offered a reasonable sounding answer:

> [o]ur minds are adopted to the small foraging bans in which our family spent ninety-nine percent of its existence, not the topsy-turvy contingencies we created since the agricultural and industrial revolutions [Pinker 1997, p.20].

Pinker then went on to characterize the accompanying environmental or natural selection pressure as "a camping trip that never end[ed]" [Pinker 1997, p.207]. So in a gross sense the demands of primitive camping were likely to have driven the development of our particular mental capabilities (or adaptations). The jump from this framework, though, to offering plausible explanations for prodigious mental capabilities is not easy to imagine.

Herein I look only at some examples of musical prodigies as described in Andrew Solomon's *Far From the Tree* [Solomon]. Solomon had opened his chapter on prodigies with the Russian classical pianist Evgeny Kissin. Kissin's mom and dad were respectively a piano teacher and an engineer, and moreover they were living as what might be characterized as Soviet Jewish Intelligentsia in Moscow. They had initially assumed that Evgeny's sister, Alla, would follow her mom and play the piano, while Evgeny would follow his dad and go the engineering route. At eleven months, though, the boy managed to sing an entire Bach fugue after hearing Alla practice it. Thereafter Evgeny pursued singing in response to just about "everything he heard". This was so relentless that his mother became very concerned about it.

Then at twenty-six months Evgeny made his appearance at the piano. He:

> sat down at the piano and with one finger picked out some of the tunes he had been singing. The next day he did the same, and on the third day he played with both hands, using all of his fingers. He would listen to LPs and immediately play back the music. "Chopin's ballades, he would play with those little hands, and Beethoven sonatas, Liszt's rhapsodies," [his mom reported]. At three, he began improvising. He especially liked to make musical portraits of people [Solomon, p.408].

He then liked to quiz his family on these portraits.

Kissin displayed exceptional skills early and eventually that led his reluctant piano teaching-mom to take him to a prominent piano teacher at the famous Gnessin State Musical College in Moscow. There at age 5, that teacher - Anna Pavlovna Kantor - would later report that:

> I saw a light in him. Without knowing how to read music or the name of notes, he played everything. I asked him to translate a story into music. I said we were coming into a dark forest, full of wild animals, very scary, and then step by step the sun rises, and the birds start singing. He began in the piano's lower register, in a dark and dangerous place, and then, lighter and lighter, the birds awakening, the first rays of the sun, and finally a delightful, almost ecstatic melody, his hands running along the keys. I didn't want to teach him. Such imagination can be very fragile [p.408].

At age 7 he began to write down his compositions. Zhenya would later state that, "[w]hen I would return from school, I would, without taking my coat off, go to the piano and play" [p. 409]. He then added, "I made my mother understand that that this was just what I needed" [p.409].

These characteristics are remarkable and certainly would seem to have been largely innate. Is it realistic to think that DNA could be behind young Zhneya's musical inclination and aptitude?

Another prodigy of note was the historical musical savant Thomas Bethune or Blind Tom [Treffert, pp.87-92]. Born in 1849 as the son of the slaves, Charity and Domingo Wiggins, he and his parents were sold the following year to General James N. Bethune in Columbus, Georgia. General Bethune then allowed the blind infant to have the run of his plantation. Although, Tom apparently had significant challenges in addition to his blindness - "[h]e was restless, explosive, and required constant supervision" [p.89], he displayed a remarkable affinity for music and more generally sound. This became apparent after his exposure to the piano playing of General Bethune's daughter. As Darold Treffert noted via a quote of Tom's contemporary, Dr. Edward Sequin:

> Till 5 or 6 years old he could not speak, scarce walk, and gave no other signs of intelligence than his everlasting thirst for music, but at 4 years already, if taken out of the corner where he laid dejected, and seated at the piano, he would play beautiful tunes; his little hands having already taken possession of the keys, and his wonderful ear of any combination of notes they had once heard [p.88].

Somehow Blind Tom from a young age could simply hear something played and play it back. Furthermore he could store it up for future usage. His ultimate repertoire was estimated as 7,000 musical pieces. He also had an analogous capacity to hear and then accurately repeat verbiage he was exposed to, despite having a personal vocabulary which may have peaked around 100 words.

Beginning at age 8 Tom became a touring sensation and as such made plenty of money for the Bethunes. In conjunction with the success of his impressive performances there were naturally those who tried to disprove or debunk his musical genius along with his staggering memory. Thus, routinely as part of his performances there was an opportunity for audience members to test Blind Tom. In one scenario at a performance at the White House the 11 year old Tom faced some skeptical musicians who played two new compositions for him. One was 13 pages in length and the second was 20 pages in length. Tom reportedly played these back accurately. Tests like these seemed to do little to debunk Tom's reputation.

Darold Treffert wrote that a general assessment, though, eventually came from a panel of 16 expert musicians. That assessment included:

> [w]hether in his improvisations of performances of compositions by Gottschalk, Verdi, and others, in fact in every form of musical examination - and the experiments are too numerous to mention - he showed a capacity ranking him among the most wonderful phenomena in musical history [p.88].

Somehow Blind Tom, although reportedly untrainable, found a way to be phenomenal musician. This despite having a career that was significantly limited to a role as a commercial vehicle for his legal guardians. The author Mark Twain was moved to attend a number of Tom's concerts and admiringly referred to him as the "archangel".

As a sample of Tom's amazing abilities, in one of his regular acts he would simultaneously sing "Early in the Morning"; play "Fisher's Hornpipe" in C with his left hand; and play "Yankee Doodle" in B flat with his right hand. Darold Treffert notes some similarities between Blind Tom's abilities and those of the contemporary musical savant, Leslie Lemke [pp.93-109]. A note here for possible followup reading is that both Blind Tom and Leslie Lemke have a number of internet sites dedicated to their stories.

An interesting contemporary prodigy story is that of the pianist Drew Peterson [Solomon, pp.417-419]. Drew somehow became an exceptional performer despite being raised in a musically-modest family. Drew did not speak until his was three and a half years old but was clearly intelligent. In fact at 18 months he managed to point to a word that his mother had skipped while reading to him. Like other musical prodigies he exhibited a remarkable sensitivity to sound.

After some informal training with his mother, Drew then went on to start formal lessons at age five. He then skipped about six months of material and ended up within a year "performing Beethoven sonatas at the recital hall at Carnegie Hall and was flown to Italy to perform in a youth festival where the other youths were a decade older" [p.418]. Eventually, Drew's parents tried to get him to have lessons with a notable teacher at the Manhattan School of Music, Miyoko Lotto. Lotto, though, was hesitant. But after hearing him she later reported:

> [h]e could barely reach the pedals, but he played with every adult nuance you'd ever want. I thought, 'Oh my God, this really is genius. He's not mimicking and not being spoon-fed. His musicality comes from within' [p.418].

On the way to kindergarten one day Drew asked his mother, "[c]an I just stay home so I can learn something"? His mom later reflected, "[h]e was reading textbooks this big, and they're in class holding up a blowup M" [p.418]. Additionally, Drew, as is common with prodigies, demonstrated enormous self-determination. In Drew's case, his parents seemed to wisely brace against the hype associated with prodigies. As Solomon pointed out, "[t]hey never expected the life into which Drew has led them, but they were neither intimidated by it nor brash in pursuing it; it remained both a diligence and an art" [p.418]. In a related contrast Solomon quoted Harvard professor of music, Robert Levin, on the lack of improvement associated with the contemporary trend of ambitious parents pushing their young pianists offspring into the terrain of demanding musical pieces [p.417].

In somewhat of a parallel, Drew's academic instincts and gifts had him halfway through a Harvard University degree at age 16 when Solomon met him. At that point Drew had related to Solomon that he had thought he might find a topic as a Harvard student that equaled or even exceeded his interest in music. But Drew pointed out that that didn't happen and "I'm not sure I really want to". Additionally, he stated "I want a life in music" [p.419].

Conceivably genetics might offer explanations for these prodigious and focused trajectories. In Steven Pinker's *How the Mind Works* after a somewhat dismissive discussion about the overlapping phenomena of geniuses -

as in they are pretty much like the rest of us - he went on to add that they may "have been dealt a genetic hand of four aces" [Pinker 1997, pp.361-62]. From a scientific perspective, though, any meaningful explanation for prodigies and geniuses would have to in large part be based on DNA. What else could provide for their exceptional smarts and inclinations? In his loose book, *From Bacteria to Bach and Back*, the philosopher Daniel C. Dennett claimed (in italics) that, *genes don't account for genius* [Dennett, p.24]. A DNA basis for high intelligence could not fully explain geniuses since there have been plenty of high intelligence individuals who didn't produce very high-level work or breakthroughs. Nevertheless, the overlap between high intelligence and genius appears to dictate that geniuses should have generous DNA contributions to their IQs. Furthermore, prodigies also tend to display strong innate drives which would appear to require additional DNA support. With genetic contributions increasingly in question this definitely adds to the mystery of prodigies and geniuses.

When reading either Pinker or Dennett you can sense denial at work. At no point do either of them look at some of the extraordinary aspects of genius, beginning with the conundrums associated with prodigies. These are inherently - and certainly from a materialist perspective - very perplexing. Why can't such super-educated authors acknowledge this? Both tried to minimize the innate aspects which is not realistic. Pinker for his part emphasized the experience or training aspect in the life of geniuses, and Dennett seemed to go further adrift to point to memes (repetitive behavioral phenomenon hypothesized to be analogous to genes in their dynamics) as an explanation. With prodigies, though, how can either approach provide realistic explanations? Very young children who appear to hit the pavement running in an adult-focused fashion are simply astounding.

Conversely, Darold Treffert whose longtime research focus has been on autism and savants has concluded that:

> I must say, though, from my observations of prodigious savants and prodigies, it appears to me that it is the actual knowledge itself within an area of special expertise that is inherited [Treffert, p.91].

And along with that knowledge you might argue that in some cases a focused determination appears to be inherited.

One final prodigy considered here is Kit Armstrong. Kit's prodigious abilities showed up early. He was able to count at 15 months. His mother May taught him addition and subtraction at age two. He then went on to teach himself multiplication and division. Solomon suggests that at age three Kit was asking about things for which the theory of relativity was required for an explanation (this claim is of course extraordinary and probably a tricky one to establish, though). Kit's mother raised him and she was not pushy. In fact she was concerned about his hyper-development and thus hoping he might "grow down" in kindergarten [Solomon, p.456].

While completing second grade Kit also managed to finish off high school math. By age nine Kit was ready to try college and enrolled at Utah State University. At ten he toured Los Alamos National Laboratory with his music manager, Charles Hamlen. At Los Alamos a physicist took Hamlen aside and told him:

> unlike the postdoctoral physicists who usually visited, Kit was so bright that no one could 'find the bottom of this boy's knowledge' [p.456].

Within a few years Kit had a residency at MIT and there he helped edit some papers in chemistry, physics, and math. About Kit's apparent ability to pick up so much information and expertise his mother simply said:

> [h]e just understands all things. Someday, I want to work with parents of disabled children, because I know their bewilderment is like mine. I had no idea how to be a mother to Kit, and there was no place to find out [p.456].

If scientists would consider kids like Kit they might share in that bewilderment.

Kit Armstrong's lasting extraordinary contributions, though, have been with his piano performances and composing career. When Kit was five years old May Armstrong wanted to find him a hobby and she went outside of her own interests and decided to try piano lessons. Consistent with his intellectual prowess Kit raced ahead on the piano. After his first lesson Kit returned home to make his own staff paper and then proceeded to attempt a composition. Solomon reports that Kit's facility with the language of music had "come to him whole" and that he could simply hear music on the radio and then "play it back" [p.456]. This is an another extraordinary but somewhat loose claim.

To connect with Kit's love of music his mom moved them to London so he could study at the Royal Academy of Music. There he became the first student of the expert pianist Alfred Brendel, a man who coincidentally also did not come from a musical background. When Kit was thirteen a journalist who was a strong critic of placing children in serious performance situations attended one of his concerts. After that performance the journalist wrote:

> [h]is playing was so cultured, his joy in performing so obvious, his commitment as he stretched his small frame to reach the low notes so total, that my objections seemed mean-spirited [p.457].

Like a number of prodigies you can read about Kit Armstrong's career on the internet.

One curious phenomenon appears amongst some these prodigy examples. That is that some of these super-bright kids would seem to have a choice between moving ahead rapidly in an academic career or alternatively in music. At least amongst this admittedly small sample of prodigies they went with music. One might then wonder if there are other individuals who could have been exceptional at music but instead chose an academic focus. I suggest that if there is a tendency to choose the music route then that might reflect something basic. Perhaps music tends to be more fun than straight intellectual work.

The realm of prodigies appears to be home to some phenomenal, science-challenging behaviors. Could evolution really have established a collection of DNA ingredients that might explain those behaviors? I find that possibility hard to fathom.

B. Unusual but Accepted Phenomena - Transgender Children

I complete my look at accepted behavioral conundrums by considering some observations of transgender people, in particular transgender children.

Some individuals strongly identify with the opposite gender and this identification can show up when they are very young. This is not a moral issue but it can raise serious challenges for the affected individuals. One way or another as human beings we tend to groove into habits and routines, and some of these are gender-based. It can also be a very frustrating situation for the affected individual in their having to live out of synch with their body-type.

This phenomena is not that uncommon and I have seen some adults who have habituated to dressing like the opposite gender. I also have encountered women who although they don't cross dress, psyche-wise really do seem like men. The intellectual question here is how could this happen? One transgender study found that amongst the subset of transgender people that have undergone sex-change surgery (or transitioned) many "knew that they had been born into the wrong gender from childhood" [Landau]. Such an explanation from the scientific perspective would seem to require some kind of DNA mutation which resulted in an individual whose brain was committed to identifying as the opposite gender, and also precociously inclined towards the corresponding behavioral agenda.

From an article in the *New York Time Magazine* [Padawer] a description of a 3 year old included the following:

> he insisted on wearing gowns even after preschool dress-up time ended. He pretended to have long flowing hair and drew pictures of girls with elaborate gowns and flowing tresses. By age 4, he sometimes sobbed when he saw himself in the mirror wearing pants, saying he felt ugly.

Such behaviors can present difficulties for the parents. As one father put it, "I didn't know how to be the father of a girl inside a boy's body".

One eight year old's self assessment found in Andrew Solomon's *Far From the Tree* contained:

> I'm a girl and I have a penis. They [her parents] thought I was a boy until I was six. I dressed like a girl. I said, 'I'm a girl.' They didn't understand for the longest time (Solomon, p.604).

This child's assessment went on to look ahead (after considering possible fixes for their penis problem) and state:

> [w]hen I'm a mommy I'll adopt my babies, but I'll have boobies to feed then and I'll wear a bra, dresses, skirts, and high-heeled shoes [pp.605-606].

Are such behaviors plausible in terms of evolution and in particular as a function of DNA specifications?

Solomon described an incident following a workshop on dealing with transgender youth. One anxious father approached the presenters with the question, "[b]ut what if he changes his mind?". One of the presenters responded with. "[y]ou just explained how he told you on the changing table at two that he was a girl, and that message hasn't changed in thirteen years". Solomon went on to conclude that it took the presenters "about ten minutes to bring this man around to an acceptance he had been unable to achieve for over a decade" [p.641]. One trans child told his parents at age

15 months, "I'm not a boy. I'm a girl". This child went on to request a Barbie doll at age two. Another trans girl at age two had a favorite pastime of wearing their mom's "red high heels, a towel on his head for hair, and anything he could drape as a sari" [p.662].

The difficulties facing trans kids including the significant risk of suicide attempts provide plenty of incentive for relevant activists. Solomon pointed out that "[m]ore than of half trans people are rejected by their families", and "even in families with some acceptance, it often comes from only one parent" [p.645]. Solomon also provided some disturbing statements made to trans children by their parents.

A September 2017 *Scientific American* article, "When Sex and Gender Collide", by Kristina R. Olson provided a more recent and science-framed overview of the trans phenomena [Olson]. In the article Olson stated about trans kids that:

> when predicting their identities in the future, trans girls see themselves becoming women and trans boys feel that they will be men, just as other girls and boys do. Even when we present children with more indirect or implicit measures of gender identity - the measures that assess reaction times rather than children's more explicit words and actions - we have found that trans girls see themselves as girls and trans boys see themselves as boys, suggesting transgender identities are held at lower levels of conscious awareness.

On gender-oriented behaviors, Olson wrote that:

> [t]he degree of their preferences for stereotypical clothes, as well as their tendency to prefer to befriend those of their self-identified gender and the degree to which they see themselves as members of their gender group, is statistically indistinguishable from their peers' responses on the same measures throughout the childhood years.

Olson added a further conclusion that:

> [a]ll of this research combines to show that transgender identities in even very young children are surprisingly solid and consistent across measures, contradicting popular beliefs that such feelings are fleeting or that children are simply pretending to be the opposite gender.

This is both a life-challenging phenomenon and also a science-challenging one. It is worth noting some points with regards to Olson's conclusions. I have seen a number of conservative political commentaries in which the phenomena is questioned because of the underlying genetic contradiction (i.e., the presence or absence of a Y chromosome should determine gender). This is certainly reasonable science-based logic and ironically it is conservatives that are often derided for ignoring the relevant science. But, whatever the prevailing intellectual beliefs are, as a parent of any child you have an opportunity to come to your own conclusions and that personal understanding might be the most significant one in guiding you with your responsibilities. One way and another kids will surprise you and the job of parents would seem to be respond as best they can to the actual situation. Instead of looking to science (or other abstract sources) for answers it might be better to look and consider for yourself, and also perhaps see what others in similar circumstances have found to be helpful.

I think that unusual behaviors like those found with the trans phenomena and with prodigies provide solid rebuttals to scientific materialism and more particularly science's understanding of human development. Within a Nature-plus-Nurture framework these phenomena appear to demand overwhelming - implausible if not impossible - Nature contributions. Thus I think that at least around the behavioral edges there are accepted phenomena that defy scientific materialism.

C. Initial Taboo Phenomena

I open here with some perspectives on taboo or paranormal research. In broad ways, Charles T. Tart's 2009 *The End of Materialism* and Rupert Sheldrake's *Science Set Free* are reasonable places to obtain overviews. Tart worked in the field of transpersonal psychology or parapsychology for many years and from that background his book attempts to overturn the position of materialism. Sheldrake, on the other hand, offers a more philosophical take in part coming from his position as kind of an excommunicated scientist. Tart's book is centered on paranormal research, while Sheldrake's goes beyond the paranormal front to consider a range of interesting taboo topics. I start here with some comments on Sheldrake's *Science Set Free*.

Rupert Sheldrake's first and I think most basic message is on the rigidity found in the scientific establishment, including its fixation on materialism (or physicalism). Sheldrake attempts to communicate that fixation as well as the idealization-prone contemporary following it has generated. Sheldrake chose the following characterization of science by the entertainer Ricky Gervais as representative:

> [s]cience seeks the truth. And it does not discriminate. For better or worse it finds things out. Science is humble. It knows what it knows and it knows what it doesn't know. It bases its conclusions and beliefs on hard evidence - evidence that is constantly updated and upgraded. It doesn't get offended when new facts come along. It embraces the body of knowledge. It doesn't hold onto medieval practices because they are tradition [Sheldrake 2012b, p.27].

Sheldrake responded to this take by politely calling it "hopelessly naive" in that it implies "scientists as open-minded seekers of truth, not ordinary people competing for funds and prestige, constrained by peer-group pressures and hemmed in by prejudices and taboos [i.e., the default human package]". In my experiences such naive characterizations appear to be quite common and this could be symptomatic of the rise of scientism. Even in my regular science readings - including *Scientific American*, *New York Times*' science coverage, and also *Union of Concerned Scientists*' literature - there appears to be a very strong tendency to view science in a largely idealized way. On the other hand, if you want critical self-appraisals (as well as humor) you are much more likely to find them in sports literature.

One of the distinguishing features of *Science Set Free* is the historical perspective that Sheldrakes provides on the workings of modern science and as part of that a number of excellent quotes are given. Beyond some coverage of psychic phenomena, his book doesn't feature that much in the way of paranormal findings - or even address the possibility of life after death - but it does consider such taboo questions as "Are the Laws of Nature Fixed?", "Is Matter Unconscious?", as well as "Is All Biological Inheritance Material?" (the latter is his aforementioned take on the missing heritability problem). *Science Set Free* appears to be carefully done and it is certainly worth a read for those interested in questioning science in big ways. One minor critical point, though, is that Sheldrake, although championing openness, left quite a number of sincere paranormal topics out of his discussions. If you want to sincerely question science (not to mention make a career of it), I think it is appropriate to at least acknowledge other analogous efforts too.

Why Science Is Wrong About Life and Evolution

Elsewhere Rupert Sheldrake did make a point of seriously investigating the hypothesis that pet dogs somehow know their owners are coming home [Sheldrake 2011] (this was also briefly touched on in *Science Set Free*). But unless you have some serious intellectual investment in denying such a possibility, would you really care about this claim? Would dog owners love and appreciate their dogs more if it were evident that these pets inexplicably knew when their owners were coming home? What is of perhaps greater significance is that Sheldrake follows thru in his appendix to recount his experiences with skeptics, including the skeptic Amazing Randi. Pet dogs may inexplicably know when their owners are coming home, but as Sheldrake notes, skeptics appear to have little interest in meaningful assessments of reports challenging materialism. In Randi's case he personally acknowledged to Sheldrake that his publicized debunking efforts of the dog investigations in fact didn't happen [Sheldrake 2011, pp.314-15]. Additionally, in its coverage of psychic phenomena *Science Set Free* also describes a number of significant exchanges that Sheldrake had with skeptics and scientists including Richard Dawkins. Scientists may project certainty with regards to the status of scientific materialism, but it appears that they very rarely bother to investigate challenges to it and thus are not adept at defending it.

Moving on to Charles Tart's large *The End of Materialism* where you can find discussions of a lot of paranormal phenomena. The book focuses on what Tart considers to be the "big five" which are telepathy, clairvoyance, precognition, psychokinesis, and psychic healing. Tart concludes that from many rigorous experiments, as well as spontaneous phenomena, it is reasonable to conclude that:

> humans [are] beings who are more than just their physical bodies, beings who can sometimes communicate mind to mind, sometimes clairvoyantly know the state of the physical world, sometimes predict an inherently (by physical laws) unpredictable future, sometimes affect physical objects by thought and intention alone, and sometimes affect, for the better, other biological systems, as in psychic healing [Tart, p.291].

Tart then suggested that these big five phenomena provide "glimpses of mind operating in this larger [spiritual] reality" [p.291]. The remaining topics in the book Tart characterizes as "maybes", and these include out-of-body experiences, near-death experiences, postmortem survival, and reincarnation.

Tart's book tries to tie these phenomena to a larger significance, in particular, that these provide evidence of our spiritual nature. I found this at times to be difficult to read as Tart seems to do too much hand-holding. This includes an excessive amount of explaining on topics like how science is supposed to work; about the differences between religion and spirituality; and about the nature our psychological tendencies and biases (Steven Pinker also tends to do this). I suggest that if the paranormal examples sufficiently contradict materialism then that should suffice in ending materialism (although don't expect scientists to take note). Making the larger connection to a deeper vision beginning with a spiritual nature, though, is not easy given the rare and/or small scope of most paranormal phenomena. Given his experimental background in parapsychology, Tart seems to unfortunately undervalue some of the truly amazing singular psychic phenomena in favor of much more modest - albeit controlled - laboratory observations.

The problem I suggest in Tart's selection of the "big five" can be clarified with an analogy. Imagine if you will that some prominent scientists were to come out and claim that our sense of humor and/or our tempers, are simply illusions. This could be quite an entertaining development, with at least the former conjecture probably being utilized as standup comic material. The thing about these qualities - our tempers and sense of humor - is that they are gross everyday phenomena and as such they are self-evident (although in the posited scenario I still imagine that some academics and intellectuals would tend to stand by the prominent scientists' denial position). Conversely, by focusing on the experimentally-observed big five, Tart's argument about ending materialism then depends on marginal phenomena which appear to have little net significance. The acceptance of such phenomena might produce nightmares for some materialists (and nominally end materialism), but it could arguably do little to change the perspective on life. Ideally, some of the well-supported examples could then gain general acceptance; scientists and skeptics might retreat to a so-rare-who-cares stance; and inevitably some intellectuals would feel compelled to wheel in some kind of esoteric physics-based explanations (very likely involving quantum mechanics which paranormal researchers already appear fixated on).

But the more significant content in a book like *The End of Materialism* might be argued to be found in reports of truly remarkable singular or spontaneous events. Tart opens the book with an apparent spontaneous breakthrough to a deeper perspective on life. This occurred in 1872 to a Canadian physician Richard Maurice Burke and it appeared to reveal to Burke a deeper transcendent perspective on life and reality. Charles Tart refers to this as an experience of Cosmic Consciousness [Tart, pp.2-5]. Tart then bracketed his book with a recent Cosmic Consciousness episode, this one involving a subsequent colleague of Tart, Alan Smith. Smith had been a physician and anesthesiologist at the time when this episode just dropped in on him. Although he described it as the "most powerful event of his life" and despite its lasting influence on him, Smith acknowledged that over time he couldn't get the experience to reoccur, despite longing for it. Episodes such as these suggest that somehow big psyche breakthroughs can show up in people's lives and have somewhat of a lasting (and in part frustrating) impact. As interesting as these may be, though, they are regrettably rare occurrences without apparent means for objective confirmation.

Another striking example which appeared to rise far above the relatively mundane plane of psi experimental results (how significant would it be to you to know that under certain blind-guessing scenarios, you are 2% or so better at guessing than expected by random chance?), involved a British medium's apparent insight into the tragic downing of a British dirigible in 1930 [Tart, pp.263-266]. The story began with news of the much anticipated maiden flight of Britain's novel dirigible, the *R-101*. This was supposed to be the dawning of a new era in transportation, one in which long ship voyages might be replaced by air travel. Some British psychics including one Mrs. Garrett had somehow intuited that this was a flight headed for disaster. Mrs. Garrett communicated her warning to the director of civil aviation at the Air Ministry more than two weeks prior to the maiden flight. That warning was dismissed, though.

R-101 then left England on October 4, 1930 at 7:36 pm. In the early morning hours of the following day the *R-101* crashed and exploded on a hillside in France. 48 people died in the crash including the wife of the director of civil aviation. Three days henceforth a previously scheduled seance involving Mrs. Garrett was held. Present at the seance was an Australian journalist, a British psychical researcher, and an expert stenographer. The prearranged goal of the seance was to contact the spirit of the author Conan Doyle who had died three months earlier. While in a trance and trying to make that connection, Mrs. Garrett:

> [b]ecame agitated. Tears rolled down her cheeks. Her hands clenched. [Mrs. Garrett's trance] voice became hurried. "I see I-

> R-V-I-N-G or I-R-V-I-N. [Flight Lieutenant H. C. Irwin was the R-101's captain.] He says he must do something about it. Apologizes for interfering. For heaven's sake, give this to them. The whole dirigible was too much for her engine capacity. Engines too heavy ... Gross lift computed badly. And this idea of new elevators totally mad. Elevator jammed. Oil pipe plugged [more technical details] ... Almost scraped the roof at Achy [an obscure railroad junction in France]. [Tart, p.264]

And then the following day in another seance session with Major Oliver G. Villiers, an Air Ministry Intelligence officer in attendance, the following was communicated:

> [as Captain Irvin]: One of the struts in the nose collapsed and caused a tear in the cover. It is the same strut that caused trouble before they know ... (sitter believes reference was to officials in Air Ministry). The wind was blowing hard, and it was raining. The rush of wind caused the first dive. And then we straightened out again. And another gust surging through the hole finished us.
>
> Attendee Villiers: Tell me, what caused the explosion?
>
> [as Captain Irvin]: The diesel engine had been backfiring because the oil feed was not right. You see the pressure in some of the gas bags was accentuated by the under girders crumpling up. The extra pressure pushed the gas out. And at that moment the engine backfired and ignited the escaping gas.

Note here is that the final observations would seemed to have been impressive for any occupant on the *R-101*.

Tart pointed out that in the aftermath of the combined tragedy and associated seance commentary that "two Royal Air Force Intelligence officers came to interview Garrett". Some of the Intelligence people apparently had thought that Mrs. Garrett was "having an affair with one of the *R-101*'s officers: there were too many correct but classified technical details in her account!". In any case, such examples are striking and also remarkable in that they used to be seriously considered by some intellectuals. The sway of science now appears to have largely eliminated that possibility.

For readers that are interested in such material you might also check out Chris Carter's very interesting *Science and the Afterlife Experience* where you can find a number of historical medium accounts, along with thorough attempts to explain them.

D. More Taboo, Mostly From Elizabeth Mayer's Accounts

I move on here to consider some more striking examples from the paranormal realm. All of these again appear to contradict science's understanding of life and thus plausible genetic support. At the very least they provide conundrums for curious people.

In the bigger look at paranormal activity here I for the most part utilize material from Elizabeth L. Mayer's excellent *Extraordinary Knowing*. Mayer's regular work had included positions in the psychiatry department at the University of California Medical Center, San Francisco, and also as an associate clinical professor of psychology at the University of California at Berkeley. Mayer's book resulted from her investigations into paranormal phenomena after an initial experience involving some help she received in retrieving her daughter's stolen harp.

In my earlier book I considered the aid she had obtained in locating the stolen harp and also some of the amazing initial reports from the remote viewing experiments held at Stanford Research Institute in Menlo Park, California. Here I will begin with some of Mayer's experiences with psychics or intuitives. After her over-the-phone success in locating her daughter's harp, Mayer then wanted to check out other individuals with purported psychic abilities. Consequently, she phoned a woman in Cape Cod, Deb Mangelus. After giving Mangelus her first name Mayer then held back any other information. Mangelus, though, after a brief pause started into some commentary:

> "[y]ou're in the middle of a decision. There are two woman involved. They're very different. One is fiery, playful, someone you can always have fun with. She has trouble with words. Maybe she's not always reliable. Fire is a big part of the image; I see the two of you holding hands around a campfire." She pauses. "The other woman is different - really different. She's very responsible. Dutiful. Orderly. The funniest thing is happening. ... I keep seeing her hands and they're clasped in her lap. I simply can't get her to unclasp her hands." [Mayer, pp.43-44].

Mangelus' commentary really jolted Elizabeth Mayer. She had in fact been struggling with a hiring decision. It came down to two female candidates for a managing director position in an arts organization. Here is some of Mayer's reflective commentary:

> [Mangelus's] description of each woman struck me as unbelievably accurate. I'd liked the first woman a lot. She seemed like she would be enormous fun to work with, though her writing samples were terrible and I wondered how she'd handle details. I'd been less drawn to the other woman. She seemed great on details, but I doubted if she ever got excited about what she was doing. She struck me as boring. Even more to the point was this: The second woman had managed to sit through our entire two-hour interview holding her hands firmly clasped in her lap. At the time I had repeatedly wondered to myself, "How can anyone possibly keep her hands so solidly clasped for so long?" [p.44].

Additionally, Mayer pointed out that the first woman (the enthusiast) had such fiery red hair that as she exited the interview Mayer had joked to her, "*Now* I know what fiery red hair really means!"

These kind of experiences were amazing for Mayer and she repeatedly concludes in her book that "*this changes everything*". It certainly strains any conceivable "jigglings and wigglings"-based explanation that I can think of, but I have a problem with "*everything*" beginning with the possibility that it may not have helped her with the hiring decision. Nonetheless, Mayer went on to conclude that through her usage of the intuitive Mangelus, and despite telling her "nothing or as close to nothing as I could consciously manage", this woman would reveal insight:

> that made me feel that she saw my life with a clarity my closest friends couldn't match, things I knew but hadn't yet recognized that I knew. They rang extraordinarily true and were also extraordinarily important. She pinpointed the central dilemmas, choices, situations, and desires in my life. [She] was somehow breaking every mold I recognized about how people achieve insight about themselves. She *knew* me. And I couldn't begin to explain how [pp.44-45].

Her subsequent experiences with another psychic, Ellen Todd, were also reported on. Here again Mayer offered no verbal introduction even though this interaction was done in person. One notable intuition was offered with regards to the very serious nature of one of Mayer's daughters. The psychic offered an explanation for this girl's demeanor based on a very difficult experience that had occurred in a previous life. Mayer was not willing to accept that explanation, but the awareness of this unusually serious demeanor and the associated challenge impressed her. Mayer concluded the session by explicitly giving Todd five names and asking her for any insight into the named individuals (amongst whom Mayer was considering collaboration). The psychic went on to comment on four of them but was stymied on one. Todd commented that it happens sometimes that I "simply couldn't find them". Mayer later went on to check on that person and it turned out they had unexpectedly died two weeks earlier.

In a final look at the work of psychics, I consider Elizabeth Mayer's account of her interaction with John Huddleston. Huddleston provided Mayer with some of his impressions about her family. Mayer wrote about his commentary, "I told John that he had been right on a lot of things, but was totally off the mark about one person". Of that person Mayer wrote, "[i]t was simply impossible for that person would do what John told me he'd been doing". Huddleston, though, responded in a "relaxed and easy fashion" that "he could sometimes be wrong", but, "he'd stick to his guns on this one". Mayer went on to write:

> [t]welve days later, I received the news. Everything that John had told me turned out to be accurate. I was as stunned as the rest of the family - but they didn't have to contend with the fact that someone had told me all about it twelve days earlier [p.51].

Another remarkable insight that would seem to suggest that at least for some people (perhaps a very tiny minority), under certain circumstances, they can obtain information in ways that defy any scientific or materialist explanation.

Another interesting aspect in Elizabeth Mayer's coverage is her inclusion of psychics' explanations for their unusual abilities. They seemed humble and matter of fact about the subtle state they feel facilitates their intuitive insights. Inaccuracies were acknowledged as possible. Huddleston' explanation stood out in part for its optimism. He said his mind state during a reading was:

> *relaxed focus*, that is the best way top describe it. There's calm, clarity, and a receptive quality. There's also a physical component, and by that I mean I'm physically centered and grounded within myself, not drifty and discorporate. I'm in communication with the client, the barriers are down, and they are very easy to see, but I don't merge with them in order to read them. This is not an out-of-body experience, in fact my state of mind is surprisingly down to earth and ordinary [pp.51-52].

Huddleston went on to second the claim that such psychic readings are "surprisingly ordinary" and "[i]n fact most people use aspects of this state of mind in their daily lives without realizing it". I disagree with this point and suggest that if this were true it should be self-evident like our sense of humor. These really do appear to be rare and remarkable occurrences.

I change over here to a different kind of phenomenon also discussed in *Extraordinary Knowing*. This one shows up in Mayer's chapter on remote viewing research and includes some practical psychic insights. The remote viewing research work considered here was done at Stanford Research Institute (SRI) and it had been initiated via some fallout from a visit to SRI by an artist and psychic, Ingo Swann. During that visit Swann had proceeded to remotely manipulate a number of shielded instruments and generally astonish some of the personnel at SRI. His initial remote viewing exercise helped establish some funded parapsychology research work at SRI. The funding eventually totaled 20 million dollars for 24 years worth of work. It initially came from the Central Intelligence Agency (CIA) [Mayer, p.106].

Some of the remote viewing experiments as one physicist put it, "were anything but ordinary and [they] just blew our minds" [p.108]. One example I considered in *A Hole in Science* involved a remote viewing exercise that seemingly failed in a large way. The coordinates given separately to two men (Swann and a retired policemen, Pat Price), both of whom claimed to possess remote viewing abilities, were seemingly of a mundane rural location. The viewers, though, went on to independently discuss an elaborate, nearby underground facility which they assumed was the intended viewing target. It turns out, as the SRI people subsequently found out from the CIA, that right next to the coordinate-designated location was a "highly sensitive underground government installation". One of the viewers even got the classified installation's name right.

The next remote viewing example considered here was national security-inspired and involved a recruit from the ranks of the U.S. Army Intelligence and Security Command, Joe McMoneagle. McMoneagle had been very successful in his military career and from his answers in a series of interviews was judged to have good potential for remote viewing. However those interviews were performed, they did appear to give a fair assessment of his potential. Joe McMoneagle in fact turned out in his new intelligence career to "produce masses of data that were really hot and totally inexplicable by ordinary means" [p.116].

In the example related here McMoneagle was given some coordinates in the Soviet Union. Those coordinates unbeknownst to McMoneagle (and likely almost everyone else on the planet) were where an enormous building was. Seemingly in the middle of nowhere that building had just come to the attention of U.S. intelligence officials. McMoneagle's:

> immediate response was that [the coordinates] identified a very cold wasteland with an extremely large industrial-looking building that had enormous smokestacks, not far from a sea capped with thick cap of ice. Later we found out the location was Severodvinsk on the White Sea. [p.116].

After seeing his initial success, the investigators gave McMoneagle a surveillance photo of the big building and asked him to try to see inside the building. Here is an excerpt from McMoneagle's retrospective account:

> I spent some time relaxing and emptying my mind. Then with my eyes closed, I imagined myself drifting down into the building, passing downwards through its roof. What I found was mind-blowing. The building was easily the size of two or three huge shopping centers, all under a single roof ...
>
> In giant bays between the walls were what looked like cigars of different sizes, sitting in gigantic racks. ... Thick mazes of scaffolding and interlocking steel pipes were everywhere. Within these were what appeared to be two huge cylinders being welded side to side, and I had an overwhelming sense that this was a submarine, a really big one, with two hulls [pp.116-117].

At that time the US intelligence community's sense was that the Soviets were building a new type of assault ship in the building. After describing some additional observations, McMoneagle added:

> I did a detailed drawing of the submarine, adding dimensions, as well as noting the canted[/slanted] [ballistic missile] tubes, indicating eighteen to twenty in all [p.117].

Somehow McMoneagle even came up with an accurate launch date (January) for the submarines. The subsequent January's surveillance photos revealed a large two-hulled submarine on the move. It roughly fit Joe's description, including the presence of twenty canted missile tubes. A look at Wikipedia offers corroboration on length, 574 feet, and also provides some insane details like the fact that each of the twenty missiles carried 10 independently targetable nuclear warheads. The name of this Soviet submarine model was Typhoon.

An amazing and seemingly sincere report of "extraordinary knowing". The presence of such skills could certainly be of interest in the foreign intelligence domain. Also at one point Joe McMoneagle described the frightening feelings that came with performing his remote viewing exercises, but these may have been modest compared to what an actual spy on location might have experienced.

I add a few simple taboo examples from my own life. I begin with one in which I had a vivid dream of someone walking into a bathroom that I was occupying. "Vivid" here implying that I can remember it the next day, which seems to happen about once a month. The dream was of a startling-type experience (I think it woke me up) and I cannot remember ever having a bathroom privacy-related dream before. In any case, the following morning I ran a Van de Graaff generator demonstration as part of a science day at a library. At the end of my stint I walked off to use the bathroom and also to change into some bike clothes for my ride home. I obtained the (small) library's bathroom key and went to do my business. That bathroom has a large self-closing door and thus is inherently secure as the occupant carries the key inside with them. While changing into my bike shorts, though, the door flung open with a well-peopled backdrop. It was a shock.

It turns out that someone had taped over the latch on the door, thus making the door un-lockable. In the immediate aftermath of this incident I commented to the library's director something like, 'I dreamt this last night'.

A more dramatic experience came in the middle of a winter night. I awoke to repeated gunshots and sat up thinking 'some people have been shot'. I rested awhile waiting for the sound of sirens but they never came. This was a unique experience for me and it could have all been a dream. For some perspective here my once- or twice-a-year nightmares are almost always academic-oriented, usually involving showing up unprepared for a class and getting clobbered with the realization of an impending exam or expected assignment turn-in. Anyway, the next day on the news there was a story about 3 people being shot and killed in their apartment. The incident was reported to be related to illegal drug activity and occurred approximately 3 miles away. The shooting was done quietly enough that no one in that neighborhood apparently heard it (perhaps muffled by loud music?).

I wondered if I had met someone - perhaps at the downtown library - and then they had been shot since it seems plausible to me that a personal connection might facilitate extra-normal communication between individuals.

Another night I had a vivid dream of driving a car and wanting to hit a woman with it. This was a very surprising and unique dream. I do not drive much and moreover can not remember having a dream involving driving a car. In fact, whilst I frequently ride a bicycle, for whatever reason, I very rarely remember having a cycling dream. This really seemed like a unique dream. In any case, later that week there was a disturbing incident involving a child whose family I am close to. This conceivably misunderstanding-beget incident, involved a couple and in particular a mother. In order to pick up the child I ended up having to drive over and meet the couple and I was at the upper limits of my anger. As a related add-on here, I effectively throttled my anger - it is not a good idea to be punching things whilst driving a car - but that throttling carried over into a too-muted response in meeting the couple. Anger is appropriate at times and in this case my limited response may have facilitated further difficulties.

A final example involved a dream in which someone I know was trying to communicate something to me. This went on for a while but I couldn't get what they were trying to communicate. This again seemed to be a unique dream. The next morning that person called me and reported that they were going to get married.

I close here with a few comments. If psychic abilities are real and somehow consistent with the scientific model then they must have a basis in our nervous system and also have some evolutionary/DNA support. I think the hegemony of science and the rigidity surrounding the materialist vision has greatly reduced the communication of such mysterious occurrences. I think such occurrences are not too uncommon but that they tend to be shelved in the modern world. This is probably more likely amongst intellectuals. This is unfortunate and I would argue is a copout. For a published example, interested readers can see the late author Peter Matthiessen's account of his remarkable and sad premonition of the coming death of his wife. It is given in the second chapter of his book, *Nine-Headed Dragon River* [Matthiessen].

But on the other hand, I also have doubts about the apparent longterm abilities of some psychics like those reported on in *Extraordinary Knowing*. I tend to think that psychic abilities just show up occasionally, inexplicable blips if you will. I guess conceivably, though, a few people might experience a sustained run of these blips. But I suspect that such blips reflect a subtle and fragile phenomena and as such shouldn't be expected. One possible exception is that some traditional beliefs suggest that sustained spiritual practices (including meditation) can boost the likelihood of ESP occurrences (although such occurrences tend to be viewed as distractions at least from my exposure in the Buddhist sphere). A small example of a possible meditational contribution to a psychic experience might be found with Matthiessen's aforementioned premonition. I have also seen claims of extraordinary abilities purported to be associated with extraordinary meditation practices, in particular in the Tibetan Buddhist literature. But even if accurate these appear to be detours from the real goals of the practices.

An additional point here is that the work of skeptics in denouncing such phenomena in my experience is not impressive. Interested readers can look up the readers' reviews at Amazon for Michael Shermers' book, *Heavens on Earth* [Shermer]. My entry is entitled "polite but easily rebutted" and it is a two star review. Shermer's work is supposed to represent serious work by a skeptic but I found it easy to rebut his coverage on the reincarnation topic. Off of taboo topics I have seen fine write-ups by Michael Shermer, but on materialism-challenging topics the coverage is predicable, not infrequently sarcastic, and also easily questioned if not rebutted. Elizabeth Mayer's conclusion about reading the skeptics' journal *Skeptical Inquirer* was that it was "like reading a fundamentalist religious tract. I found the journal dismayingly snide, regularly punctuated with sarcasm, self-congratulation, and nastiness, all parading as reverence for true science" [Mayer, pp.93].

E. More Taboo from Mark Gober's Upside Down Book

I add some more taboo commentary based on a 2018 book, *An End to Upside Down Thinking: Dispelling the Myth That the Brain Produces Consciousness, and the Implications for Everyday Life* [Gober]. The book appears to have been carefully researched and written by a newcomer, Mark Gober. In large part it represents Gober's survey of paranormal research findings. I found it to be a good review book but it also contained some reports that were new to me.

Before getting to a few paranormal highlights I feel compelled to open with a general criticism, though. Gober's most fundamental point - which he opens the book with - is that there is a case for arguing materialism in reverse. That is, as given in his caption for an alternative pyramidal depiction of reality:

> consciousness is fundamental and everything else (e.g., physical matter and the universe ... and even brains) come from, and is experienced within consciousness [Gober, p.xxi].

This conclusion reminds me of the title of another book, *Atheist Overreach* (by Christian Smith). Gober appears to have gone from some remarkable and credible paranormal phenomena and then concluded that consciousness creates "everything else". This is a gigantic extrapolation. Why not simply let these mysteries be communicated as is and then readers can wonder about them? And how would concluding that consciousness creates everything change a person's mindset? Someone might then start pursuing positive thinking in a big way (and good luck with that).

On somewhat of a parallel if you read physicists' and/or astronomers' assessment of the significance of their own usually speculative and often remote research topics, you can find their own overreach. This tends to show up at the end *Scientific American* physics articles (for a black hole-flavored reverential example readers can look at the August 2012 issue of *Scientific American* and see "The Benevolence of Black Holes"). Gober's overreach I think overlaps with that found in other paranormal researchers' big picture assessments. Additionally, such assessments tend to involve taking what appears to be casual comments by physicists' on the nature of reality (usually based on quantum speculation and perhaps alcohol consumption) and taking them seriously.

But aside from an oversized hypothesis Gober did a nice job of laying out some of the paranormal situation. It is rather analogous to Mayer's *Extraordinary Knowing*, although missing the personal connections found in that book and also missing an acknowledgment to her fine book (this unfortunately appears to be typical as her very good book appears to be rarely cited within relevant literature). One notable thing that Gober included was copies of official declassified U.S. government assessments of SRI's remote viewing work. In one of these documents a science panel consisting of Dr. Donald M. Kerr (Director of Los Alamos National Laboratory), Dr. Fred Zacharaison (physics professor at California Institute of Technology), and W. Ross Adey (Chief of Staff, Research Division, Veterans Administration Hospital) produced a "Principal Findings" document stating (in capital letters) that:

> IMPLICATIONS ARE REVOLUTIONARY

MERITS CONTINUED FUNDING IN THE NATIONAL INTEREST

EVIDENCE TOO IMPRESSIVE TO DISMISS AS MERE COINCIDENCE

LACK OF PHYSICAL MODEL DOES NOT PRECLUDE EXISTENCE

INITIATE A FIVE-TO-TEN YEAR PROGRAM

INVOLVE ADDITIONAL LABS [Gober, pp.71-72].

Another positive conclusion came from the prominent physicist, Freeman Dyson. It was given in the preface of *Extraordinary Knowing* and there Dyson wrote that "ESP is real but belongs to a mental universe that is too fluid and evanescent to fit within the rigid protocols of controlled scientific testing" [Mayer, p. xi]. Furthermore, Dean Radin in his book *Real Magic* also presents some similar declassified assessments [Radin, pp.218-220].

While the evidence for such extraordinary phenomena appears to be very strong, the denial by the scientific establishment is easily a match. Trailing that denial appears to be the dutiful work of skeptics in dismissing any claims that challenge materialism. Gober discusses a little in his book about the reign of a group of skeptics at Wikipedia and interested readers can look up the dismissal of remote viewing there. From my own limited experiences in attempting to contribute to Wikipedia, it appears that any new content which challenges scientific materialism will be quickly removed.

I close here with mention of two remote viewing examples given in *An End to Upside Down Thinking*. The first involved efforts by the government to locate a downed Soviet Tupolev-22 bomber aircraft in Africa. Satellites at the time could not find the prized bomber so eventually a remote viewing request led Joe McMoneagle to attempt to find it. In the words of physicist Russell Targ:

> Joe was given a large map of Africa on which he could try to match and record his mental pictures as they emerged. The first thing that he saw on his mental screen was a river flowing north. Working with his eyes alternately open and closed, he followed the river until it flowed between some rolling hills. After a half-hour's work, he drew a circle on the map and said the plane was between the river and a little village shown by a dot. Within two

days, the TU-22 was found by our ground forces within the circle that Joe had drawn [p.66].

President Jimmy Carter later confirmed the success of this remote viewing operation in a speech to Emory College in 1995 [p.66].

The second interesting remote viewing exercise occurred in the law enforcement domain. After citing a report suggesting that there had been some remote viewer usage in about one hundred police departments in the United Stated, Gober gave a concrete example with regards to the Patrica Hearst kidnapping. His account begins when:

> [t]he Berkeley [California] police contacted the Stanford Research Institute, asking for psychic assistance on the matter. [Pat] Price was a remote viewer in the program at Stanford and was [willing] to help. His initial psychic impression was that the kidnappers did not want money, and instead, the kidnapping was political in nature. The police showed Price hundreds of unlabeled mug shots, and he picked out three ... Price noted that one of the men "recently had his teeth pulled out at the dentist without anesthesia, relying instead on self-hypnosis".
>
> Two days later, the kidnappers contacted the police, and, as Price predicted, they claimed that they didn't want money; instead they wanted food for the poor. Eventually, police determined that the three men Price picked out were indeed three of the men in this group. Police even confirmed Price's story about the kidnapper's dental incident [p.207].

This viewing by Price was performed about 50 miles away from the kidnappers location. Additionally, in Elizabeth Mayer's book it was pointed out that prior to his enlistment with SRI, Price had been a policeman in Burbank, California. Price claimed to have utilized what he called "ESP" during his career and also that it had led to "some of his most spectacular successes as a police commissioner" [Mayer, p.109].

I conclude this chapter by pointing out that it is easy to find sincere reports of behavioral phenomena that contradict the narrow-minded scientific/genetic visions. It is not to scientists' credit that they cannot acknowledge this. Additionally, it is not to the credit of religious individuals that they likewise tend to ignore these mysteries. Perhaps the unfolding heritability impasse will get more people to exercise some curiosity about such reports.

In the final chapter I will expand my consideration of taboo or paranormal phenomena.

Chapter 3 - The Spirit of Scientism - Steven Pinker

This chapter focuses on the work of Steven Pinker, in particular his 2013 *The New Republic* essay, "Science Is Not Your Enemy: An impassioned plea to neglected novelists, embattled professors, and tenure-less historians" [Pinker 2013] and also parts of his 2018 book, *Enlightenment Now: The Case for Reason, Science, Humanism, and Progress*. I will start with his essay as it captures a number of the problems with scientism as well as Pinker's thoroughly confident presentation.

From what I have seen, no one has directly challenged the materialist vision that Pinker's article lays out and most of the official reviews tend to find nuance-level complaints (although they may be strongly worded). I will endeavor to minimize nuances here and instead discuss the gross shortcomings along with the unfortunate persuasiveness of Pinker's writings. I will begin by chronologically critiquing points made in Pinker's essay.

A. Science-Centered Idealism

Before diving into a critical look at Pinker's essay, however, I want to open with a clarification of my use of "science" here. By this term I am specifically addressing fundamental, largely academic, science. This subset of science is centered on the subjects of biology and physics, and is for the most part a non-applied intellectual pursuit. These two subjects are charged with the tasks of investigating what physical processes are responsible for life and what physical processes have defined the universe, respectively. The physical processes responsible for life are of course assumed to be a subset of the processes considered in physics. Furthermore, there are a number of academic areas or departments that have directly inherited biology's materialist vision, including neuroscience and also psychology (the latter being Pinker's home).

On the other hand, there are many other areas affiliated with science, including applied fields like chemistry, climatology, geology, and meteorology: but this is not where my critical attention lies in this book. The attention here is on what might be called pure science, largely the domains of biology and physics. The assumptions of physics have become the assumptions of biology and thus scientific materialism and its large contemporary neo-religious import.

Steering back to "Science is Not Your Enemy", Pinker dives right into his science-promoting by claiming that notable thinkers of the Enlightenment period - famous individuals like Hobbes, Locke, Hume, Rousseau, Descartes, Leibniz, and Descartes - "were scientists". Thus we are informed that the supposed intellectual juggernaut of modern science has a prominent and broad intellectual background. I have seen others appear to authoritatively question Pinker's historical interpretation of the Enlightenment and its significance, but I will postpone this point for now. Pinker went on to acknowledge that these earlier purported scientists were handicapped since:

> [t]he mathematical theories of information, computation, and games had yet to be invented. The words "neuron", "hormone", and "gene" meant nothing to them.

The "theories of information, computation, and games" are not followed up in the essay, and that is appropriate as they appear to have only a very loose connection to the understanding of human experience, and might be more at home in the "Research Interests" listing of a Computer Science or perhaps ambitious Psychology professor. This pattern of over-inflating the science balloon appears to be a regular occurrence in Pinker's works.

The stretching continues with the introduction of "neuron", "hormone", and of course "gene". Efforts to understand ourselves has led science to put together theoretical models of life and our psyches, and the worth of the associated ingredients is no more than the confirmed veracity of those models. In the year following Pinker's essay there was a review article on the state of neuroscience in the March 2014 issue of *Scientific American*. That article, *The New Century of the Brain*, by Rafael Yuste and George M. Church provided a sober assessment missing from Pinker's neural hype. Yuste and Church claimed that:

> [d]espite a century of sustained research, brain scientists remain ignorant of the workings of the three-pound organ that is the seat of all conscious activity. Many have tried to attack this problem

by examining the nervous systems of simpler organisms. In fact, almost 30 years have passed since investigators mapped the connections among each of the 302 nerve cells in the round worm Caenorhabditis elegans. Yet the worm-wiring diagram did not yield an understanding of how these connections give rise to even rudimentary behaviors such as feeding and sex. What was missing were data relating the activity of neurons to specific behaviors.

They went on to point out how superficial and deceptive many popular presentations of human brain experiments tend to be. Their comments about superficiality appear to fit Pinker's essay in that they suggest perhaps a century of very hard work ahead (assuming the assumptions of materialism hold up) in contradiction to Pinker's subsequent claim that:

> [t]his is an extraordinary time for the understanding of the human condition. Intellectual problems from antiquity are being illuminated by insights from the science of mind, brain, genes, and evolution.

The faith in genes espoused by Pinker was in fact already staring at very dark clouds. Some geneticists were referring to DNA's "dark matter" as an ambiguous reference to the source of our missing heritability.

Pinker then went on to mock what he sees as prevalent critiques of science, and in particular the label "scientism". Pinker futzes around with the term and shows little appreciation for its gist. I suggest that "scientism" here roughly refers to a combination of two aspects of modern science. First, there is the hype and arrogance regularly associated with science. This can naturally bother people and I suggest Pinker in no small way rides on this hype wave. Secondly, there is science's total confidence in the materialistic model of life. Although, few officially want to take on materialism, I think it is underlies a good deal of the frustration with science which is captured by the critical term "scientism". As was mentioned at the beginning of Chapter 1, almost no one seemed to criticize the genetic determinism expressed in Mukherjee's *The Gene*. Never mind the empirical failures unfolding in genetics, most people are pulled along by the contemporary aurora of science, and perhaps simply want to avoid looking stupid. But underneath this I think the position of materialism and its intellectual hegemony bothers a lot of people, including some of those Pinker targeted with his *The New Republic* article.

Indirectly, though, Pinker seems to acknowledge this deeper point with his later writing that science's position:

> is not the dogma that physical stuff is the only thing that exists ... [since] [s]cientists themselves are immersed in the ethereal medium of information, including the truths of mathematics, the logic of their theories, and the values that guide their enterprise.

These points appear to be both an erroneous and a pretentious detour. The information glorified here simply characterizes pure abstraction, or in a more meaningful way, physical stuff. In the latter case, I doubt people will feel better about their themselves because science claims that they're quantifiable. The pretentious content here involving purported truths, logic, and values - like quite a bit of Pinker's writing - come off a bit like they are coming from a gung-ho graduate student.

I find it awkward to read some of Pinker's exposition. He claims that:

> In making sense of the world, there should be few occasions in which we are forced to concede "It just is" or "It's magic" or "Because I said so". The commitment to intelligibility is not a matter of brute faith, but gradually validates itself as more and more of the world becomes explicable in scientific terms. The processes of life, for example, used to be attributed to a mysterious elan vital; now we know they are powered by chemical and physical reactions among complex molecules.

This is scientism and it is simply faith-based. That it all makes molecular-only sense is certainly a dogma for science and it is too bad that Pinker can state this without drawing some flack. They don't "know" this, they believe and defend it vigorously and the unfolding DNA deficit should have more people questioning that belief. As some of the examples in the previous chapter make clear it is not hard to very seriously challenge science's molecular-only vision, although it seems nearly impossible to get mainstream scientists to acknowledge this.

Naturally, coupled with science's molecular-only view of life, is the dismissal of other perspectives. Pinker points out that:

> our minds are prone to illusions, fallacies, and superstitions. Most of the traditional causes of belief - faith, revelation, dogma, authority, charisma, conventional wisdom, the invigorating glow of subjective certainty - are generators of error and should be dismissed as sources of knowledge.

So what are we left with? Pinker provides an answer with:

> we must cultivate work-arounds for our cognitive limitations, including skepticism, open debate, formal precision, and empirical tests, often requiring feats of ingenuity.

He might well have added, "an allegiance to science", as the gist here is that to learn about the world we need the scientific method and with it to bracket our investigations down to materialism. This is coming from a psychologist who does not note that psychology's science-styled, experimental-based approach has been dogged by an inability to reproduce their outcomes (i.e., the replication crisis [Yong]). And I would further suggest by its inability to come up with significant findings.

A more basic point here is that each of us has to learn about life through direct subjective experience. Who but an intellectual is going to want to scientifically verify many of their personal observations? This point that much of the experience of life is inherently personal and subjective, and also *non-repeatable*, undercuts the assumptions and ambitions of psychology and moreover scientific vision of life. Readers might think of significant events in their lives and consider how reproducible they were. How about acts of genius or falling in love? This doesn't appear to register with Pinker.

Pinker furthers his points by directly addressing religion. He claims that:

> [t]he moral worldview of any scientifically literate person - one who is not blinkered by fundamentalism - requires a radical break from religious conceptions of meaning and value.

Indirectly Pinker is making a basic point here and it appears to be a defining point for scientism. Essentially he says 'any non-moron of course follows science and rejects religious beliefs'. And this is supposedly consistent with the claimed openness and commitment of science to tests its own perspectives. Never mind that science could well be afflicted with the very common tendency to rigidify and/or is simply caught up in its own "invigorating glow of subjective certainty". These kind of idealizations about science should probably be viewed as warnings signs.

On a more subtle point here, from my limited purview on official religions I do not think it is uncommon for them to acknowledge and even question some their basic beliefs. For science on the other hand, it appears to be very rarely done. This was why when the Nobel laureate Francis Crick wrote a book entitled *The Astonishing Hypothesis: The Scientific Search for the Soul* supporters of science like Pinker were apparently stunned. Crick's book would have been better titled, *Materialism Eliminates the Soul - Duh*, as that is what it amounts to, and "astonishing" appears to be in fact an "obligatory" for scientists. As Daniel Dennett wrote on this point:

> [t]here was nothing astonishing about this hypothesis; it had been our working hypothesis for decades. Its denial would be astonishing, like being told that gold was not composed of atoms or that the law of gravity didn't hold on Mars [Dennett, p.15].

On Pinker's point that religious views are "factually mistaken" as shown by the "findings of science". He goes on to instruct us that:

> [t]here is no such thing as fate, providence, karma, spells, curses, augury, diving retribution, or answered prayers - though the discrepancy between the laws of probability and the workings of cognition may explain why people believe there are.

The latter point is a consolation floated to believers. We can of course assure ourselves that Pinker has carefully investigated these points.

The fact that our religious faiths really do appear to have a science-observed innate basis is not mentioned by Pinker. In fact from interviews with young children it has become apparent that kids are somehow born with a faith in a spiritual aspect of life. In the 2012 book, *Born Believers - The Science of Children's Religious Belief*, Justin L. Barrett presents some of the growing evidence that infants tend to possess an innate understanding of the existence of souls/God/gods, to be believers in what Barrett called a "natural religion" [Barrett]. *Born Believers* contains some surprising examples including ones in which atheists' positions were rebutted by their young children. As Barrett wrote "[c]hildren are prone to believe in supernatural beings such as spirits, ghosts, angels, devils, and gods during the first four years of life" [Barrett, p.3]. He later added:

> Exactly why believing in souls or spirits that survive death is so natural for children (and adults) is an area of active research and debate. A consensus has emerged that children are born believers in some kind of afterlife, but not why this is so [p.120].

Sticking with the prevailing dogma, though, Barrett had these striking findings simply folded back into materialism. Even as a practicing Christian, Barrett concluded that these are simply delusional tendencies derived from evolution and nurture - "biology plus ordinary environment".

How such beliefs could have arisen out of our evolutionary journey and ultimately been stored in DNA, is difficult to see though. At the beginning of the book Barrett did offer a form of religious explanation that had been provided by an Indian man he met on a train. In Barrett's words that man had explained:

> [T]hat on death, we go to be with God and are later reincarnated. As children had been with God more recently, they could understand God better than adults can. They had not yet forgotten or grown confused and distracted by the world. In a real sense, he explained, children came into this world knowing God more purely and accurately than adults do [p.2].

The fact that we are born with a spiritual perspective should be more commonly known and wondered about.

Steven Pinker's pitch for scientism is not a short one, even if printable in only 12 and a half pages. His continues with:

> [t]he facts of science, by exposing the absence of purpose in the laws governing the universe, force us to take responsibility for the welfare of ourselves, our species, and our planet. ... the scientific facts militate toward a defensible morality, namely adhering to principles that maximize the flourishing of humans and other sentient beings. This humanism, which is inextricable from a scientific understanding of the world, is becoming the de facto morality of modern democracies, international organizations, and liberalizing religions, and its unfulfilled promises define the moral imperatives we face today.

This broad moralistic flourish - as one reviewer once put about Pinker's writing it "never runs short of hubris or hyperbole" - misses some easy contradictions. As was mentioned earlier, astronomers are still facing a decades old conundrum that 95 percent of the universe is unaccounted for. Further in the astronomical arena is the pervasive mystery as to how we got a universe like the life-supporting one we can observe (hopefully without bailing out to the omni-explanation involving many many universes). I doubt that Pinker's certainty is consistent with the conclusions of curious astronomers.

Pinker's moral claim is both dubious and central to his work and also to humanism. Even if materialism prevails there could be many points to hash out with regards to helpful priorities. As a simple rebut to the "militate"'s associated with the findings of science, one need only look at the priorities of science and try to square them with the maximal "flourishing of humans and other sentient beings". A number of years ago I followed the issues associated with nuclear weapons and the associated policies closely. In doing so it became apparent that behind the activism scenes was a significant presence of physicists. I think this was in response to discomfort associated with the contributions of physicists to the production of nuclear weapons, and also to the super remote nature of the contemporary physics research agenda. On the latter point, climate change has also been a clear concern for a number of decades now and why haven't physicists made it a significant part of their research agenda? How many physics departments in the last 30 years have made more of an effort to understand (the complex and challenging) terrestrial climate dynamics than those of other planets? How does this square with addressing the "moral imperatives we face"?

On another basic point, is it really apparent that people on board with Pinker's humanistic vision are more humane than others? By "humane" here I am looking beyond tending to vote for Democrats, read the *New York Times*, and being a big fan of science.

Pinker continues with his adulation for science in claiming:

> [i]f one were to list the proudest accomplishments of our species ... many would be gifts bestowed by science. The most obvious is the exhilarating achievement of scientific knowledge itself. We can say much about the history of the universe, the forces that make it tick, the stuff we're made of, the origin of living things, and the machinery of life, including our own mental life. Better still, this understanding consists not in a mere listing of facts, but in deep and elegant principles, like the insight that life depends on a molecule that carries information, directs metabolism, and replicates itself.

Again this does not seem justified, beginning with the closing point on the assumed functioning of DNA. Additionally, there must be some physicists who would argue against Pinker's claim about having a good grasp of "the history of the universe, the forces that make it tick". Likewise, I would hope that there would be plenty of neuroscientists questioning the assertion here about being able to "say much" about "our mental life".

Pinker then goes on to describe the "sublime beauty" associated with scientific images. As a personal response to this I have to say that when I want to see sublime beauty I don't look at scientific images. Instead I go outside for a walk or visit an art gallery. This from a technically-educated, scientifically-literate person who is comfortable with abstract concepts but not beholden to them. As a suggested test for readers you might try reading through the research interests listed at a biology or physics departments' websites. How much of the intelligible content there do you have any interest in? Do you think that looking at some associated images would prod you "to contemplation, [and] deepen [your] understanding of what it means to be human and of [your] place in nature"? I would suggest a distinctly different route to contemplation (and joy), you might spend more time outdoors and/or around young children.

A prominent recent example which offers some reasons for questioning science was the death of the physicist Steven Hawking. Central to his work was trying to understand the dynamics of black holes. In the follow-up to Hawking's death there were naturally assessments of his intellectual accomplishments. In one such assessment his work was described as mostly involving the investigation of "the information paradox" associated with objects falling into black holes. The paradox is a subtle one in which theorists have wondered about the loss of information or history associated with the devouring of objects by black holes. In particular, if the process was purely one way how could you determine a black hole's consumption history? In the currently accepted theoretical sense the record associated with a black hole's consumption of objects should be available, yet that seemed to contradict the present understanding of their dynamics. This topic and Hawking received plenty of attention, at least in some educated circles. Yet the topic is unbelievably remote and theoretical, as well as of course speculative. Nonetheless, in our scientism-skewed era even some people looking for religious insights or simply deeper meaning have looked to the writings of Hawking for guidance. Like Einstein, he at some point wrote something nominally relevant to the concept of a God (and of course was also supposed to be super smart). But what can you really do with black hole speculation? And how smart is it to spend your career studying black holes?

Pinker's article goes further in crediting science with many of our historical successes. At no point does he acknowledge that part of the legacy of scientific efforts is that it has in fact unfortunately contributed to two large problems. The first is that humanity is currently overwhelming the biosphere and with it compromising our own chances for a healthy future. Cleverness - even cleverness directed towards prolonging human life - is not necessarily a net good thing for us and certainly not for nature. Additionally, from following climate change news and research findings for years my impression is that much of the serious work has been done at the margins of academia. How much of a bow can academic science legitimately take for what little progress has been made in addressing our sustainability crisis?

The second problem here is that science has largely nuked serious consideration for alternative and/or religious perspectives of life. There may be plenty of reasons to consider such possibilities - a personal favorite of mine is the amazing innate abilities of some kids - but this is simply denied by science. There could well be more significant (as well as interesting) mysteries to mull over than the information paradox associated with black holes. Is there any secular educational institute in our country that in any official way questions materialism? In my admittedly one-way communications with philosophers I have not sensed any. Technically, you might consider the University of Virginia's Division of Perceptual Studies. That division bills itself as:

> the oldest and most productive university-based research group in the world devoted exclusively to the investigation of phenomena that challenge current physicalist brain/mind orthodoxy – including investigation of phenomena directly suggestive of post-mortem survival of consciousness.

But I doubt they are integrated at that university let alone more generally into academia. Their birth was due to external private funding, coincidentally from my home of Rochester, New York.

In "Science is Not Your Enemy" Pinker went on to claim that human:

> impulses ordinarily operate beneath our conscious awareness, but in some circumstances they can be turned around by reason and debate. We are starting to grasp why these moralistic impulses evolved; how they are implemented in the brain; how they differ among individuals, cultures, and sub-cultures; and which conditions turn them on or off.

Is this even remotely accurate? Readers' might remember the earlier official assessment from behavioral genetics [Horgan 2014] which included the phrase, "[a]s a result the psychiatric and behavioral genetics literature has become confusing and it now seems likely that many of the published findings of the last decade are wrong or misleading and have not contributed to real advances in knowledge". Pinker's writing appears to exhibit a rather selective optimism.

The latter portion of his "impassioned plea" to the humanities consists of some proposals for the possible integration of science into the humanities. It does seem likely that some ambitious humanities investigators will go with this science-ifiation flow, but is it a good idea? Does trying to find ways to introduce scientific methods and terms into non-scientific work really help? If Pinker could travel a bit further back in time (past the Enlightenment era), what kind of benefit would William Shakespeare have obtained through having words/concepts like "neuron", "hormone", "gene"; and perhaps the whole modern humanist backdrop to work into his writing?

Pinker offered some specific integration ideas. He wrote that:

> [t]he visual arts could avail themselves of the explosion of knowledge in vision science, including the perception of color, shape, texture, and lighting, and the evolutionary aesthetics of faces and landscapes. Music scholars have much to discuss with the scientists who study the perception of speech and the brain's analysis of the auditory world.

But would this really be an aid in the artistic process of finding elements that work for human psyches, beginning with the artist's own? As a simple example when I go to view art at a gallery I try to not to read anything including the title information on the pieces. Pause and take in the piece, perhaps move little forward or backwards, and see how it registers. How could an artist's efforts to intellectualize the production process through science, or my own in viewing it, really be an improvement?

He went on to offer a suggestion with regards to utilizing the successes of behavioral genetics so as to offer "profound implications for the interpretation of biography and memoir". Next, he made plugs for the "cognitive psychology of memory" and the "social psychology of self-presentation". Would this really be useful even if these cited fields were anywhere near as accomplished as implied? Conversely, do the humanities really have anything to directly contribute to scientific work?

I am offended by the logic of Pinker's work. His research work in studying the acquisition of past tense verb forms - or for that matter modern research into the minute physical details at a place like CERN - has very little to do with the current practical efforts associated with science (and for counterarguments involving the trickle-down practical fallout from pure science work, those should be balanced with consideration of comparably funded, practically focused efforts). Finally, science really isn't a big team effort, the different fields are largely independent of each other. Thus there is no singular entity, science.

B. Some Existing Reviews of Enlightenment Now

Steven Pinker's 2018 book, *Enlightenment Now: The Case for Reason, Science, Humanism, and Progress*, followed up on his earlier book, *The Better Angels of Our Nature: Why Violence Has Declined*. These books together build lengthy cases in support of an optimistic appraisal of the humanity's trajectory, in large part due to the efforts of "reason, science, and humanism". I would suggest that the mostly positive responses to these works is both a statement of the contemporary allegiance to science (and probably also to Pinker), and also indirectly a reflection of current anxiety levels.

Here we have an apparently brilliant academic (and certainly a highly-skilled writer) backed by our supposed supreme vehicle of comprehension - science - and he is essentially giving a big thumbs up to our trajectory. I disagree with a number of points made here but will get started with a few reviews of others. First, on the positive side we have Bill Gates who said about *The Better Angels of Our Nature* it is "[t]he most inspiring book I've ever read". *The New York Times* characterized the same book as "[a] supremely important book". On the subsequent *Enlightenment Now* book Bill Gates ratcheted up his previous claim with, "[i]t's my new favorite book of all time". For the most part customer reviews for these books are also very positive and which might reflect the pretty common adulation of science.

Now to consider problems with these works I first turn to some critical customer reviews of the latter, *Enlightenment Now*. It turns out there that were a number of critical reviews including about 14 percent of the Amazon customer reviews being one star reviews. When there is that kind of negative review presence for a significant book by a celebrity - let alone a science-affiliated celebrity - that is noteworthy and I think worth some review-reading time. From my review-scanning experience such books tend to be reflexively greeted with 4 and 5 star customer reviews and seeming applause.

I will start with a review submitted on February 23, 2018. In it the author identifies some of Pinker's selectivity in supporting his enlightenment case beginning with his optimistic take on the impact of science and technology. He points that scientific and technical efforts by the Germans were very significant contributors to the horrors of World War II. Further this reviewer generalized to assert that just as science has contributed to positive outcomes it has likewise facilitated negative ones too. That reviewer also pointed to (as did others) China's not very enlightenment-oriented policies being a big contributor to some of the developing world's positive statistical trends.

I add a followup point along the population front. China's one child policy in no small way appeared to help arrest their population crisis and thereby facilitated the transition of many Chinese out of poverty (a neighboring counterexample can be found with India). Likewise Pinker cites the down swing in Iran's fertility without mentioning that this largely followed incentives-based government policy measures. Pinker overlooks the basic point that population pressures are a very big deal in the modern world and ironically this situation is significantly a result of humanity's success in increasing longevities.

The additional customer review I consider here is actually a two star review and was submitted April 15, 2018. This appears to be the work of a scientifically- or technically-trained person. The casual style of Pinker's writing obviously offended them. The reviewer suggested that this book was written for readers who are "willing to trust the author as an expert or authority and will not engage in any [or very little] critical thinking of the author's claims". The reviewer was also offended by Pinker's use of "appeal to authority" for arguing points. I add that Pinker's larger authority here is the idealized entity, science. That reviewer also was offended with Pinker introducing the concept of entropy in *Enlightenment Now* and suggested that Pinker "clearly has a very limited understanding of dynamical systems". I would furthermore question whether any actual expert in entropy (which is an inherently subtle but significant physical characteristic with an intellectual home in the field of thermodynamics) has ever written a big book trying to extrapolate this concept into something psychologically or socially significant? I hope not. Pinker's use of entropy appears to be simply science-flavored, intellectual ornamentation.

The same two star reviewer went on to point out that "[c]areers are now being built on attacking religion and spreading atheistic doctrine, and some of this is reflected in the pages of this book". They also question whether someone's religious affiliation - specifically attending church once a week - really qualifies for downgrading them to "religious" versus "scientific" status. The reviewer, a self-proclaimed atheist, says from his own observations this does not make sense. The reviewer then went on to add a conclusion paragraph:

> From a scientific point of view therefore the book is very disappointing, even though the intentions are good. The lack of a self-critical attitude, the lack of humility in the face of complexity, the frivolous name-calling, and the uncritical adulation of authority makes this book one that would take considerable revision to

make it a viable case for technological and moral progress, and would swell its page count way beyond what it currently is.

I consider one more existing review of *Enlightenment Now*. A formal review was published in the February 22, 2018 issue of *Nature* and was entitled "Testing times for optimism" [Goldin]. The reviewer, Ian Goldin, is an economist and professor of Globalization and Development at Oxford and has authored books that overlap some with the terrain of *Enlightenment Now*. Golding opened his review with some historical comments including that "[m]any of the breakthroughs that Pinker attributes to the Enlightenment [period] actually pre-date it". He then pointed out that the "Renaissance was a period of even more dramatic progress in science and humanities" and furthermore that before this period there were many scientific insights uncovered, and that some were uncovered in non-European locations (and likely in redundant fashion too). On that final point, Rupert Sheldrake pointed out in his *Science Set Free* that "at least six hundred years ago, some Arabs and Chinese were inoculating people with material taken from the pustules of others suffering from a mild form of small pox" [Sheldrake 2012b, pp.262-263]. That historical point on the long ago advances towards fighting small pox was taken by Sheldrake from an immunology textbook. Pinker neglected this point in his presentation.

After pointing out some of the downsides to the Enlightenment period Goldin went on to suggested that "science and evidence-based reasoning do not necessarily triumph over irrationality and ideology". Goldin then wrote that "[s]hared social norms and ethics are the framework that allows reason to prevail". This point on shared norms is very significant as these reflect cultural factors and I follow-up on this point in some detail later.

On a big basic point, Golden says that "[e]conomic growth has come at the expense of ecosystems" and that:

> Pinker does cite climate change, but as a worrying exception to a relentlessly positive narrative, rather than as the most glaring example of a wider failure of global commons management.

One can certainly criticize Pinker's mostly singular focus on global warming by considering the large scale makeover humanity is carrying out on the biosphere. Also the book's optimistic pitch that our increasing efficiency of means has reduced our environmental footprint is misleading. Even with improvements in efficiency we are still gnawing away at nature and it is the overall or net impact that deserves attention. The famous historical principal that Pinker neglects here is the Jevons Paradox (named after a

British economist, W. S. Jevons). Jevons had written (in italics) with regards to British coal usage in 1865 that:

> *It is wholly a confusion of ideas to suppose that the economical use of fuel is equivalent to a diminished consumption. The very contrary is the truth.*

Individuals can certainly find ways to reduce their energy usage by switching to more efficient devices, but the net or society-wide impacts of such improvements have unfortunately tended to increase energy usage [Owens]. Our energy efficiency challenge is to find and use more efficient devices, whilst not offsetting this with increased the device usage.

One technical marvel that Pinker touts is the development and production of synthetic nitrogen-based fertilizer. He doesn't mention that this development has also managed to double the amount of nitrogen fixation in the biosphere and that this is its own sizable environmental threat [Smil 1997]. As the researcher Vaclav Smil pointed out, with regards to nitrogen fertilizer we have developed a "profound chemical dependence" and movements to minimize it - including "[a]n early stabilization of population and the universal adoption of largely vegetarian diets" do not look "particularly likely". The subsequent 22 years has born out this out.

Goldin's review in *Nature* concludes "that *Enlightenment Now* is not a balanced account of the present or future", but on the positive side "for the many overwhelmed by gloom, it is a welcome antidote".

C. An Unenlightened Review of *Enlightenment Now*

I go on here to provide some additional criticisms and comments on Pinkers' 2018 book. I concentrate here on several weak points in *Enlightenment Now* and these include a realistic look at our environmental/sustainability crisis; an accounting for of the cultural obstacles hindering improvements; the impact of our increasing slide into electronic distraction and physical inactivity; and a realistic look at the mysterious Flynn Effect. These I suggest are sizable deficiencies in Pinker's vision, a vision in which an emphasis on reason, cleverness, and an allegiance to science (along with a rejection of religion) provide a sufficient basis for optimism and progress.

Before jumping into a sustainability critique, I offer an example which I believe is related to Pinker's sustained anger towards the Left. Years ago

I would venture out occasionally for these monthly organized bicycle rides. These were relaxed group rides around the city of Rochester in part simply as casual celebrations of city cycling. At one point a serious liberal activist joined us for the ride. As the group began riding along a large city street we were organized into a one lane wide pattern. This left free the other same-direction lane for passing autos. Well, it turns out this wasn't sufficient for the accompanying activist. This guy was apparently offended at the acquiescence to auto traffic so he tried in solo fashion to block passing autos. This led to a dramatic and dangerous incident with an irate driver. I can still vividly remember the incident and the fact that even some of our group's very polite older lady cyclists really lost their composure. It was an insane move by the activist guy.

And where was this guy coming from? As far as I could gather he was a PhD student who was significantly plugged into the intellectual vision/mission that comes in part from Pinker's work vicinity of Boston, Massachusetts. That vision is espoused by *Z* magazine and people like Noam Chomsky (a former MIT colleague of Pinker's) which has a found a home in taking academia's politically correct blinder-ed purview as a basis to attack any implied form of injustice and repression (one of their latest e-mail opens with "[a]fter 54 years of non-stop radical involvement ... [wanting to do] a podcast about vision and strategy for massive social change"). I think this type of over-the-top academic-related activism really bothers Pinker and thus the recurrent axe-grinding in this and other writings. Another irritant to Pinker has to be the terrible legacy of Communism which was seemingly born from neighboring humanistic and intellectual impulses.

I get started with Pinker's casual treatment of humanity's impact on nature. Instead of using what appears to be some optimistic opinions on the status of endangered species, he should have provided some wholesale numbers. Relevant estimates are available for example in works like "The biomass distribution on Earth" by Yinon M. Bar-On, Rob Phillips, and Ron Milo [Bar-On *et al* 2018] and also others by Vaclav Smil, including his "Harvesting the Biosphere" article (or book by the same name) [Smil 2015]. Comprehensive works like these are necessarily complicated in having to make comprehensive estimates of historical quantities, and also include very tiny life forms. Nonetheless, they represent very important work. In Bar-On *et al* many relevant conclusions can be found beginning with "the mass of humans is [about] an order of magnitude [10x] higher than that of all wild mammals combined". The authors point out that our innovations have led to growth in human populations that "have had radical ecological effects". Amongst birds the total mass of domesticated ones (primarily chickens) is now three times that of wild birds. On historical trends, Bar-On *et al* cite the work of Barnosky which suggests that the contemporary total weight of wild mammals (both terrestrial and marine) is about one-sixth that of their pre-human exposure level. By including the mass of humans and our livestock in that comparison, though, it goes from a loss by a factor of six to a gain of about a factor of four. There are some very significant estimates in their paper.

Bar-On *et al* went on to point out that:

> [a] worldwide census of the total number of trees, as well as a comparison of actual and potential plant biomass, has suggested that the total plant biomass (and by proxy, the total biomass on Earth) has declined approximately twofold relative to its value before the start of human civilization. The total biomass of crops cultivated by humans is estimated at 10 Gt [carbon-based biomass in gigatonnes (billions of metric tonnes)], which accounts for only 2% of the extant total plant biomass.

Given the size of that missing biomass - representing roughly 500 Gt of carbon - it is relevant to our climate crisis. The principal cause of that crisis is annual human-based emissions of about 40 billion tons of CO_2, which corresponds to about 10 Gt of carbon. If Earth had not lost so much of its tree-based carbon sequestration it certainly would have helped.

Consistent with these points the gross threat established by humanity's growing presence was officially acknowledged the following year in the 2019 UN report on biodiversity. That report was produced by the Intergovernmental Science-Policy Platform on Biodiversity and Ecosystems Services and their very comprehensive report ran 1,800 pages! For focused reading the 40-page summary for policymakers is available [IPBES] and it contains a succinct sober introduction missing in *Enlightenment Now*. The summary points out that, "[a]round a million species already face extinction, many within decades, unless action is taken".

Pinker also takes shots at the ecological inclinations of indigenous people. He states that as humans get better educated and richer, they tend to care more about the environment and are more active in trying to preserve it. He also wrote that:

> [w]hen native peoples first step foot in an ecosystem, they typically hunted large animals to extinction, and often cleared vast swaths of forest. A dirty secret of the conservation movement is that wilderness preserves are set up only after indigenous peoples have been decimated or forcibly removed from them, including the national parks of United States and the Serengeti in East Africa [Pinker 2018, p.123].

Pinker should have tried to quantify this and might simply have offered a bar graph roughly describing the historical gross decline of nature. On the left could have been a bar representing the cumulative decline up to the Enlightenment period and on the right the subsequent decline. I think that such a bar graph would strongly contradict Pinker's optimistic take on modern trends. Additionally, another apt bar graph comparison could utilize contemporary deforestation estimates for the Amazonian rainforest. One bar could represent the annual losses in acreage due to the actions of indigenous peoples and the other due to the efforts of modern people (driven in large part by modern meat-eating habits). Would the indigenous deforestation bar even be visible? An important point buried here is that whatever we modern people say in polls may in significant part simply reflect self-conscious reflexes to trendy intellectual and/or social pressures.

Pinker claims that the long frustrated wait for nuclear fusion to become available for energy production "really may be thirty years away (or less) this time" and used citations from *Time* and *Bloomberg News* [Pinker 2018, p.149]. He also makes a big point of highlighting the climate-friendly potential of traditional atomic (fission-based) energy. In part his pushing of fission energy appears to be taking a shot at some traditional environmentalists who still oppose it. The corresponding environmental movement Pinker attacks as being irrational "greenism", which he broadly characterizes along with some right-wing movements as:

> secular religions, providing people with a community of like-minded brethren, a catechism of sacred beliefs, a well-populated demonology, and a beatific confidence in the righteousness of their cause [p.32].

Pinker later goes on to more specifically attack greenism as an "apocalyptic movement" which is:

> laced with misanthropy, including an indifference to starvation, an indulgence to ghoulish fantasies of a depopulated planet, and

Nazi-like comparisons of human beings to vermin, pathogens, and cancer [p.122].

But is Pinker's favored environmental movement, ecomodernism, just another secular religion which has its own agenda which could be in no small way be to simply rebut the traditional environmental movement? Additionally, has an ecomodernist center like the Breakthrough Institute produced any breakthroughs? I add here that a traditional big environmental organization - and the one with what has to be the largest presence of scientists - is the Union of Concerned Scientist (UCS, coincidentally headquartered in Cambridge, Massachusetts) and they have for a long time championed the need for a critical look at nuclear power safety (I have supported them and followed their literature for decades). Is UCS a greenist organization and are their safety concerns bogus?

I felt a personal connection with regards to the book's casual treatment of our energy challenges. In the past I followed closely these issues and prepared for a graduate education and possible career in that area. I located a department which was very active in facing this long term predicament. They had researchers trying to improve fission options, investigate fusion options, and also help inform intelligent energy policies. I then spent a year studying there and in so doing confirmed their commitment and concurrently the difficulties posed by these problems (not the least of which is simply getting the government to commit to helpful policies). My own personal situation led me to return to Rochester, but nonetheless it was a very valuable experience and gave me a firsthand sense of some of the serious longterm commitment present on our unfolding energy/climate challenge (albeit on the margins of academia).

My detour into sustainability-related studies is quite relevant to Pinker's presentation. The department I was in was MIT's Nuclear Engineering Department, the same institution that housed Pinker at the time (he is now up the street at Harvard), and the time was 1986. Instead of concocting an anti-greenism skewed portrayal of our climate challenge, he could have sat down with people who have researched and lived with these topics for decades and offered readers a serious take on what our options appear to be. Having an interview portion in his book also would have diminished Pinker's over-placement of himself as an authority.

During that detour into sustainability studies I had the good fortunate of encountering the work of Vaclav Smil. Smil did a PhD thesis long ago entitled "Energy and the Environment: A Long Range Forecasting Study" and his subsequent thorough research work has largely stayed in that neighborhood (although he largely moved away from forecasting). Smil has been described in an interview with *Science* magazine as "perhaps the foremost thinker on energy of all kinds" and as "the man who has quietly shaped the way the [informed] world thinks about energy" [Voosen/Smil 2018]. He has been described by Harvard's energy and climate scientist, David Keith, as "a slayer of bullshit" and his ability to debunk the prevalent "hopey-feely going on in the energy policy community" impressed University of California at San Diego's climate policy analyst, David Victor [Voosen/Smil 2018]. His work has alway impressed me as being super thoroughly done. Pinker doesn't even mention Vaclav Smil, or as far as I can tell, other informed sober perspectives in his energy/climate coverage.

Instead of appealing to pure intellectual optimism with:

> [t]he human mind with its recursive combinatorial power can explore an infinite space of ideas, and is not limited by the quantity of any particular stuff in the ground [p.127].

Pinker could have noted that careful analysis leads to what might be termed the simple sober option. Here as given by Smil:

> High-income economies simply have to find ways to reduce their average per capita energy use, such as by cutting their extraordinarily high food losses (about 40%), and [reducing] their wasteful transport. Such actions would increase well-being and improve trade balances as well, while steadily reducing CO_2 emissions.
>
> We should not forget that the environmentally least disruptive action is not to turn to new technical solutions to produce more energy in different ways, but simply to do with less. "Less is more" has never been more desirable than the case of tackling the rising levels of atmospheric CO_2.

Smil elsewhere has also pointed out the big dietary savings available (beyond limiting food waste) by reducing meat consumption. This approach of personal commitment and adjustments appears to be frowned on by Pinker in favor of pursuing technical developments.

Somewhat consistent with his preferences for technical fixes, in 2019 Pinker co-authored a *New York Times* opinion article entitled "Nuclear Power Can Save the World: Expanding the technology is the fastest way to slash greenhouse gas emissions and decarbonize the economy" [Pinker 2019]. There are certainly reasons to preserve and possibly enhance nuclear's electricity-generating contribution (currently at about 20% in the

United States), but saving the world is certainly a stretch [UCS Nuclear]. The *New York Times* nuclear article doesn't even provide overall numbers on how enhancing nuclear capability would contribute to rolling back global emissions. A basic point here is that globally only 17 percent of (primary) energy consumption is directed towards the production of electricity [Smil Chase]. We can not "save the world" by largely eliminating emissions from a 17 percent piece of our energy consumption pie.

Pinker also makes light of the vegetarian potential and claims that livestock only make a 5.5 percent warming contribution. So his stated 15 percent land-use warming contribution has little to do with animal husbandry? The estimates I have seen for meat eating's contribution to global warming are approximately 15 percent and assessment's like the aforementioned 2019 UN report naturally highlight the big environmental costs associated with our heavy reliance on animal husbandry. Official estimates have it that about 50 percent of the planet's habitable land is occupied by agriculture and that about 77 percent of that is in turn occupied by livestock. Those livestock only provide about 17 percent of humanity's supply of calories and about 33 percent of its supply of protein. Vaclav Smil, by the way, is not a vegetarian but this hasn't stop him from pushing these points and also adjusting his own diet.

Somewhat consistent with the gist of Pinker's vision of big climate change-motivated transitions has been Germany's large effort, the *Energiewende*. That ambitious push has made little headway, though:

> [i]n the year 2000, when Energiewende began, Germany derived 83.7% of it primary energy from fossil fuels, in 2015 that share declined to 79.4%. Average decline has been merely 0.3%/year and its continuation would leave fossil fuels dominant even by 2050. And there have been other surprising outcomes. Germany's consumption of poor-quality Braunkohle (lignite) burned to generate thermal electricity had actually slightly increased between 2000 and 2015, while the burning of natural gas, the cleanest and least carbon-intensive fossil fuel, had decreased by about 10%. Because of the falling overall primary energy use, Germany's 2000-2015 decline in fossil fuel consumption was about 12% in energy terms, but France, Germany's neighbor that has no equivalent of Energiewende, reduced its reliance on fossil fuel by about 18% during the same period. So much for the unequaled success of Energiewende [Smil Transitions 2016].

Even in a very competent technical society like Germany, a society in which almost a minority are nominally religious [Pinker 2018, p.489], the government orchestrated transitions have been frustrating. And from the intellectual breakthrough perspective that Pinker appears to espouse, he might have mentioned that the very deep-pocketed and intellectually-loaded Google "launched its 'Clean Energy 2030' in October 2008, aiming to eliminate U.S. use of coal and oil for electricity generation by 2030, and cut oil use for cars by 44 percent" and that program "was completely abandoned in November 2011" [Smil Revolution 2015].

Unfortunately, even the relatively enlightened traditional diets of Spain and Italy, the so-called Mediterranean diet, have declined in usage. The average Spanish diet has gone from about 20 kg of meat per year in 1975 up almost 100 kg, whilst the Italians now consume almost as much which is roughly triple the amount they did 50 years ago [Smil Addio]. The historical drift of modern diets has not been a smart one or consistent with Pinker's optimistic take on the "natural consequence[s] of people's preferences" [Pinker 2018, p.144].

Additionally, Pinker's optimistic take on those preferences does not seem consistent with the contemporary auto production spectrum. We now have compact cars with over 300 horsepower (see for example the Honda Civic Type R) as well as "13 vehicles packing more than 700 horsepower you can buy today, fully warranted and from established automakers" [Stoklosa]. Contemporary motorcycles are no slouches either with at least 10 production bikes producing around 200 horsepower or more [Simon]. It is worth remembering that "horsepower" can be taken literally.

If readers have not read some of Vaclav's work then I recommend trying it. At his website he even has a number of downloadable articles available. The short ones including those from the engineering magazine *IEEE Spectrum* are outstanding. You can easily get a lot of basic information and the presentation appears to be minimally afflicted with the axe-grinding tendency common in academia. On a related point, Bill Gates has stated that he awaits the next Smil book "the way some people wait for the next *Star Wars* movie" [Voosen/Smil 2018]. That might not be a good approach, though, as Gates apparently did not digest Smil's findings which are for the most part contradictory to those in *Enlightenment Now* (which is Gates' current favorite book). I also add that Gates' enthusiasm for *Enlightenment Now* appears to be self-serving as Pinker is effectively singing the praises of technical developments which Gates's life/philosophy is heavily invested in.

Finally, I must applaud Pinker's discussion on the geo-engineering option. For some this option has been strictly taboo but that does not appear to be a realistic. Pinker points out that the journalist Oliver Morton in his book *The Planet Remade* makes a reasoned case for the use of "moderate and temporary" geo-engineering given the challenges associated with climate change. I would add that given the fact that some heavily populated areas in the world are already seriously heat-challenged [Fischetti] I think the push to consider geo-engineering options could quickly grow. Additionally, the Arctic vicinity is leading the relative warmup dynamic and given the positive feedbacks in place up there (warming tends to accelerate the melting of ice and snow which in turn leads to additional warming) this could further motivate geo-engineering consideration. It is worth noting that geo-engineering is one relatively novel intellectual frontier (unlike coming up with new energy sources), and that a significant push in this area could help us buy critical time on the climate crisis. We should try to place all of our options on the discussion table. I still fondly remember the Mt. Pinatubo eruption and its subsequent global cooling effect.

I move on to another topic which I believe is neglected in *Enlightenment Now* and that is culture. Although Steven Pinker has on occasions acknowledged his admiration for the work of the economist and author, Thomas Sowell, I have yet to see him incorporate the most basic message coming out of Sowell's work. That is that culture can be a very significant factor in human progress and wellbeing, and furthermore that naive corrective actions tend to be problematic. A big relevant example in *Enlightenment Now* is Pinker's optimistic assessment of the status of African Americans and the associated issue of racism. Although, Pinker likes to think of himself as a "watchdog for politically correct dogma in academia" I will suggest here that he is still largely blinded by that correctness. Moreover, I suggest that that correctness package is somewhat of a moral sibling or counter-balance to scientific correctness, and it is held pretty thoroughly by academics including - and contradicting Pinker - scientists. It is also championed by secular entities like the *New York Times* and also the "humanistic" Unitarians.

I get started with Pinker's analyses of the prevalence of racism in our society. He does so by citing the work of the economist Seth Stephens-Davidowitz investigating internet searches for jokes involving the n-word. The study concluded that such searches are on the decline but still noted that they are apparently mainly coming from "white men", although the "main exception was a sliver of teenagers" [Pinker 2018, p.218]. I offer my own contrary evidence gathered while living in the city of Rochester, New York, where as of 2010 our population breakdown included 43.7 and 41.7 percent, white and black portions, respectively. Across roughly 35 years I have heard white individuals use the n-word 5 times, including once in anger and directed towards an African American. On the other hand, I have heard that word used routinely, and not infrequently in anger, by young African Americans. I doubt the older African American man I saw at a post office wearing his "Retire the N-Word" hat was doing so out of concern over internet searches involving n-word jokes.

The above is a simple introduction to the sway of political correctness (PC), beginning in academia. I would be surprised if Seth Stephens-Davidowitz bothered to consider the pretty ubiquitous usage of the n-word amongst young African Americans, or that quite a bit of apparent racial animosity could have an underlying cultural/behavioral basis. I also doubt Stephens-Davidowitz would have considered investigating intergroup violence rates as a sober measure of possible racism (intergroup crime rates between black and white individuals are heavily skewed towards white as victims [Williams Who Are]). Additionally, I am reminded of the recent PC outcry over the presumed sexism of the old song "Baby, It's Cold Outside". In response, some of the Readers' Picks comments in the *New York Times* pointed out that somehow the lyrics in rap music get a pass.

Pinker lays out evidence that African Americans are doing well and this of course fits a basic point in *Enlightenment Now,* that is that in a gross sense all boats are rising together. Pinker pointed out that contemporary illiteracy amongst African Americans is "effectively zero percent" and that in recent history "they have been getting much happier". The contrary point is regularly made by African American critics like Thomas Sowell, Walter Williams, and Larry Elder. Their most basic point is that African American family structure has greatly declined under liberal policies and in particular illegitimacy rates have risen from roughly 11 percent in 1938 to a current level of over 70 percent [Williams, Blind to]). Additionally, such critics claim that a relatively weak commitment towards education and a tendency towards violence are still substantial problems in parts of the African American community. Much of what I have seen locally has been consistent with that critical take and contrary to Pinker's (and academia's) optimism.

I begin with a simple example to highlight cultural problems prevalent in parts of the African American community. In an *NPR* article entitled "What Really Happened at the School Where Every Graduate Got Into

College" the followup on a successful year at a high school in Washington, D.C, was recounted [McGee]. That school, Ballou High School, had all of their seniors graduate and get accepted into college. The graduation ceremony in June 2017 had been a celebratory affair and the lead up to that ceremony had included national media coverage. Yet in the aftermath a contradictory story broke out. Some Ballou teachers pointed out "half of the graduates had missed more than three months of school ... unexcused"; when they did attend many "often need[ed] intense remediation"; one teacher reported that a significant number of the students "couldn't read and write"; and that moreover the process was simply "smoke and mirrors". Additional reports mentioned that "kids just roamed the halls with impunity" and that the minimum assignment score had artificially been set to 50 (even for missed assignments).

The actual Ballou achievement numbers (amongst test takers) were aligned with the above critical takes:

> 9 percent of students there passed the English standardized test. No one passed the math test. The average SAT score ... was 782 [with the minimum and maximum scores possible, 400 and 1600, respectively].

The *NPR* story, presumably like any other mainstream media coverage, had to present this as a local mishap which had victimized the overwhelmingly African American student body (currently the school is listed as 97 percent black). To their credit, though, *US News and World Report* mentioned that "the same pattern is evident in districts across the nation" [Malkus]. I think the standout fact in Ballou's scandal was that there were apparently no students or parents who protested this educational farce. The actual protestees as depicted in the NPR article were some African American teachers who likely experienced humiliation on their jobs. Additionally, I suggest that readers might keep the above 50 minimum score in mind when encountering reports on improvements in urban African American educational achievement.

I suggest here that this mishap was representative of a much larger culturally-driven problem and that it underlies a good chunk of the contemporary racial unrest. Pinker appears to be unaware of this. Many African American kids - certainly in cities - do not appear to be onboard with a commitment to learning but there is enormous politically correct/liberal pressure to pretend around this (as well as the associated behavioral problems). As a result many of these kids are simply fake-graduated and passed along to inevitable humiliation, perhaps at college, where one of Ballou's ambitious students acknowledged he had had "reality slapped in [his] face". Walter Williams succinctly examined this problematic affirmative action-assisted scenario in his fine article "Cruelty to Black Students" [Williams Cruelty to]. That article gives some basic achievement numbers and in conclusion states:

> [t]he average black 12th-grader has the academic proficiency of a white eighth- or ninth-grader. Consider the following question: If one admits 1,000 randomly selected eighth- and ninth-graders to college and also admits 1,000 randomly selected 12-graders, who do you think is going to come out on top? Would you be surprised if the eighth- and ninth-graders felt inferiority, oppression and insensitivity?
>
> The academic elite feel righteous seeing blacks on campus, even if they are severely mismatched. Black people must ask: Are we going to sacrifice our youngsters so that white liberals can feel good about themselves?

I add some local experiences relevant to this situation. When my son was a first grader in one Rochester's elementary schools I did some volunteering and also would pick him up after school. Three incidents happened there that year that clarified some key aspects of contemporary urban cultural challenges. One involved a young male teacher sprinting across the school's playground and leaping the fence in very impressive fashion to breakup what appeared to be an assault on an African American student by some other African American boys. A second incident involved myself observing what appeared to be a white boy insulting an African American girl. It appeared as if could have been along racial lines so I took off after the boy. He lived close by and managed to beat me to his house. Subsequent contact with the school's very dedicated principal, though, let me sit down with the boy's father and the principal. The father was very apologetic and the incident seemed resolved. The dedicated principal likely followed up with the insulted girl as well.

The upshot from these incidents is what is lost in the modern academic-led discourse. From what I have seen there is a lot of sensitivity about traditional racism amongst whites and moreover the net flow of group-to-group help locally is clearly from whites to African Americans. My son's class involved a lot of white volunteer assistants in the form of the teacher's church friends (which I believe was in a largely Republican-voting suburb).

The ongoing liberal/academic narrative neglects this. Also minimized is the very big problem of violence in parts of the African American community. One of our high schools recently recorded 700 fights in a year. One of my African tutoring assistants sadly reported about her (different) high school "there are fights everyday".

But the third and most significant event I observed at my son's school came when a fellow parent pointed out the advanced or college preparation-oriented sixth grade class, which happened to be standing outside at the time. That class was approximately 50 percent African American and 50 percent other (mostly white) which appeared to match the school's demographics. Together, with my concurrent observations of affirmative action at college and the news that the city's top high school would end its objective test-based admissions policy, this was a real jolt. The previous test-based admissions outcomes had been deemed "too elite" (to their credit New York City's public schools still have some "too-elite"-based admissions policies). Shortly, thereafter I attended a school meeting and stood up to suggest that such artificial admissions distortions are in no way helpful. This - not surprisingly to me - drew the ire of a white, apparently liberal parent. Now a little over twenty years later our top high school has had its academic rating decline to 3 out of 10, after posting 9-ish out of 10 examination results in the early 1990's. Many of our high schools have (greatschools<dot>org) academic ratings of 1 or 2 out of 10 (for additional context, Ballou high school's rating is currently at 2 out of 10). And beneath this I would suggest is the combined influences of weak educational commitments apparently quite common amongst urban African Americans, plus the substantial sway of liberal idealism. Academics like Pinker might object some to the excesses of affirmative action at college but the larger problematic impact associated with affirmative action can be found in public schools systems with significant African American populations. The push to at minimum eliminate appearances consistent with traditional racism - academically and discipline-wise - has caused big problems in such systems. A notable irony is that in the nominally bad old days there were fine, and of course demanding, all-black public schools [Williams Discrimination and; Williams Black Ed].

This cultural rut is readily apparent in person. In 9 years of volunteer tutoring students, almost exclusively from our city's public schools, I have found that overall non-African American black students (from their own diverse cultural backgrounds) seem to be about 10 times more likely to show up for tutoring help or simply some additional work, than are African

American students. The backdrop here is that the former constitute about one tenth of the latter's population. If you follow your group's tendencies and punt on education then you are making your life much more difficult. Culture is apparently a huge factor here and moreover the select group outcomes-drama focus of academics neglects this. Pinker's claim of 100 percent literacy amongst African Americans is challenged by what a Rochester library official confided to me. They reported that tests indicated that about 40% of our adult population was "functionally illiterate".

I add some additional culture-related observations, mostly as seen in the *New York Times*. The *Times*' is overwhelming a traditional liberal/academic-consistent publication but inadvertently balancing their perspectives are frequently the contributions of their readers. On topics like affirmative action and the need for economically integrated housing (or in particular making Section 8 housing more available in middle class neighborhoods) the readers (as implied by the Reader Picks selections) will often strongly contradict the *Times*' positions. These contrary comments are usually based on personal experiences, but in the case of affirmative action it seems that about half of them are simply philosophical in nature (i.e., 'Affirmative action is racist - period.'). The critical response to affirmative action was strongly captured in the *Times*' coverage of efforts to introduce affirmative action into New York City's elite high school admission practices (see for example the comments on [Shapiro (1)]).

To see some of the comments is to sample what academics do not see and with this some of the limits of Pinker's academic or Enlightened "data". In a recent article on difficulties facing some urban charter schools the comments from the public school realm were revealing. One Reader Picks comments included:

> [d]iscipline is one thing we don't have in the NYC public schools where I teach. In my elementary school, children are allowed to do what ever they want because the schools are penalized for reporting violence, both student-on-student and student-on-teacher (And, the children know this)[.] The mayor and chancellor can sugar coat it with publicity visits and photo ops, but that's not what's happening in the real world of our schools.
>
> We have children (five years old) screaming in the halls, rolling on the floor, hurting other children, and six adults trying to get

them calmed down. We're not allowed to say anything or do anything. And those children, by law, must be admitted to the school [unlike in some charter schools or any athletic program]. Parents refuse responsibility for their children's behavior and teachers are unable to teach. It's heartbreaking for those children who do have respect for education and want to learn. They are overshadowed by the unruly and disrespectful. Our funds are limited for the professionals we need for counseling and family services [Shapiro (2)].

The point here is that what is really happening, if it is sufficiently taboo - including critical perspectives on African Americans - is simply not allowed entry into official discourse. Another series of critical perspectives were present in the Reader Picks comments on an article about San Francisco's efforts to desegregate their public schools [Goldstein]. I have watched in amazement and dismay as a number of refugee kids that have I tutored over the years received A's and A+'s, along with glowing comments, largely for being nice kids. The fact that disruptive kids are disproportionately African American seems to have stymied disciplinary actions and as some African American critics have pointed out, this has ironically hurt ready-to-learn African American kids. Unless someone like Steven Pinker actually spends time in some of these schools then they will never know about these situations and thus get a glimpse of the true extent of academic/liberal distortions on race.

The scholar Thomas Sowell hypothesizes that the cultural difficulties experienced in parts of the African American community were in part picked up in part from the redneck or cracker culture that was prevalent and problematic amongst whites in the South (and before that whites in the lawless regions of the British Isles) [Sowell]. Whatever its origins, habits involving being overly aggressive and maintaining weak educational commitments are problematic and deserve attention.

A general suggestion here is that culture is an important global challenge, although from reading *Enlightenment Now* (or science journals) you would not know this. From the overall problem of adjusting humans to the unfolding sustainability crisis, down to particular challenges like prioritizing learning, culture is a big hurdle (and prime example of human rigidity). In his earlier enlightenment-oriented book, *The Better Angels of Our Nature*, Pinker had rebutted the cultural concerns of the very interesting book by Gregory Clark, *A Farewell to Alms*, by suggesting that "when institutions change, a nation can vault itself to spectacular rates of economic growth"

[Pinker 2011, p.621]. And how often has that happened? It would be nice if many of the struggling developing countries could rapidly stabilize and more ahead, but I think that is unlikely without a lot of internal and ultimately personal struggle. I think that that is where a lot actual progress happens. In any case, within the United States the plight of African Americans - and with it the state of a number of our cities - do not appear to have fulfilled Pinker's progressive take despite plenty of financial help and humanistic input.

I move on to another challenge facing the modern world and one neglected by Steven Pinker - and that is the increasingly non-physical and electronically-distracted norms of our lives. I begin by describing a couple that I spent some around, my grandparents. My family would visit them at least a couple of times a year at their rural residences in Pennsylvania (mostly the last one in Stewartstown). They lived perhaps relatively unenlightened lives. They lived in small minimally electronic-ed residences and did quite a bit of their labor manually, including growing and preparing some produce. They were quite outdoorsy and I can still remember going for long walks with my grandmother (who didn't seem to mind hard shoes). They were not overweight. They also read regularly and kept abreast with the news via periodicals. Consistent with this they were concerned about global issues, although environmental concerns were just beginning to register. Their house and car were kept very clean. Their car's seemingly ever-new state always amazed me. They were Republicans. They were what might be described as 'old school' including being religious. My grandfather was a Presbyterian minister. They probably followed some science but certainly did not worship it. They lived relatively simple lives.

In a basic way I suggest their lifestyles were somewhat of a complement to that praised by Pinker. Coming from a different background I couldn't understand some of their preferences including a ban on cursing, but they seemed to easily accommodate me. I look back on my grandparents here because I think their lives highlight a number of problems facing the modern, increasingly tech-influenced world that *Enlightenment Now* praises. Even in today's world I doubt they would have surrendered much of their attention to electronic screens or their physicality to the modern conveniences that seem to plague us. I think that the simplicity of their lives if adopted in the modern world could be quite helpful. At one point in Vaclav

Smil's writings he endorsed the idea of people in the developed world embracing energy consumption akin to the average Frenchman in 1959. My grandparents' energy consumption might well have qualified.

I now fast forward to my recent experiences in tutoring. Almost all of the students that I see are refugees (simply because they show up). I get to see a wide variety of cultures and consistent with this tend to form those dreaded generalizations or stereotypes. It is natural to make them - on average groups really do differ - although in personal interactions the generalizations recede. But a big dynamic that I see challenging *Enlightenment Now*'s optimism is that many of the refugees, beginning with the kids, become sedentary; put on weight; spend an enormous amount of time glued to screens; and I suspect become depressed. The differences between their lives and the corresponding hard-working outdoorsy upbringings of some their parents is simply stunning. This could be worrisome for a number of reasons, including the wellbeing implications. On the other hand, the remarkable work dedication of some of the refugee parents that I've encountered may well help them stay afloat. The fact that this questionable modern dynamic is neglected by Pinker is revealing. If the bottomline is an adherence to intellectual/secular-religious principles you could well underappreciate some important aspects of life.

In a December 2018 *Scientific American* article entitled "Kids These Days: A looming crisis and how to avert it" the skeptic Michael Shermer cites some official academic warnings arising over the impact of electronic devices and social media [Shermer 2018] . Citing the work of San Diego State's Jean Twenge reported on a number of growing trends with regards to the occurrences of mental difficulties amongst the Internet Generation (iGen). This cohort began entering college in 2013 and during the period between 2011 and 2016 reports of self-injury amongst college students rose by 30 percent. Additionally, suicide rates increased between 2007 and 2015 for 15- to 19-year-olds by 46 percent. Shermer reported that Twenge found:

> a positive correlation between the use of digital media and mental health problems. Revealingly, she also reports a negative correlation between lower rates of depression and higher rates of time spent on sports and exercise, in-person social interactions, doing homework, attending religious services, and consuming print media, such as books and magazines. Two hours a day on electronic devices seems to be a cutoff, after which mental health declines.

Shermer then went on to cite some of the work of Greg Lukianoff and Jonathan Haidt presented in "The Coddling of the American Mind" suggesting that our slide into electronic distraction - along with hyper concerns about feelings - has led to an increasing mob-like internet landscape. I have not seen Pinker acknowledge any of this which should be a self-evident and obvious concern. The large and growing displacement of our attention to video screens should in fact be an obvious worry even without any official scientific declaration. (And for people questioning Twenge's statistics [Denworth], I would in turn question any serious statistical analyses given the difficulty in finding controls (i.e., kids with minimal screen exposure).) How much of our real life do we want displaced by screen-viewing? How much electronic communication and physical passivity is enough? Significant critical perspectives on such points routinely show up in the comments at the *New York Times*.

I go a bit further with lifestyle trends here. One of the big complaints among academics and liberals is our growing economic inequality. The other growing inequality I suggest is one between those still living physically active lives and the growing segment of sedentary individuals. One can observe the enormous amount of time spent on electronic screens these days and in parallel you can observe the increasing lack of fitness in our society. We have become increasingly diverted from physicality and the outdoors. In a gross sense this is visible with the increasing presence of obesity, and in a subtle sense with the lack of fitness and also good posture (spending a lot of time with your neck bent down to stare at your cell phone is a prescription for neck difficulties). Jared Diamond made the point of the changing physiques he observed in New Guinea with the spread of modernity [Diamond]. Well, we are way deep in that process.

I continue with the decline in physicality to suggest a general point. If there had been some ongoing academic focus on improving the fitness of Americans - analogous to the big pushes to enhance learning and diversity that goes on in education departments - then I think it quite likely that such physical fitness academics would have tended to imagine the success of their programs. Then such positive appraisals might have been utilized by someone like Pinker to tout as another modern intellect-led triumph. A number of the optimistic points in *Enlightenment Now* - including the positive appraisals of our psychological well-being, the pending medical breakthroughs, and the purported boon that has been cell phones and social media - are appraisals that seem very one-sided. Furthermore, the comments in the *New York Times* (and for brevity again the associated Reader Picks' ones) often strongly contradict the *Times*' politically/academically-correct positions. Who has more credence with regards to the impacts of cell phones on the lives of teenagers, someone who has taught high school for thirty years or an intellectual with a techno-optimism agenda?

I move on to make one final point. As in his earlier book, *The Better Angels of Our Nature: Why Violence Has Declined*, Pinker cites the rising trends in intelligence (or IQ) tests as broad evidence of humanity's progressive trajectory. He even goes on to connect this rising phenomena (officially the Flynn effect) with the decline in religious faith. Specifically, he wrote that:

> we have already seen that better-educated countries have lower rates of [religious] belief, and across the world atheism rides the Flynn effect: as countries get smarter they turn away from God [p.438].

Before addressing the mysterious Flynn effect I pause here and point out that this reasoning misses an alternative dynamic. That is that modern educational systems almost inevitably do not question science, and in particular materialism, which of course tends to unseat religious perspectives. Moreover scientific education - like spokespersons such as Pinker (and Harris to follow) - often arrogantly convey a sense of certainty in their presentations. The alternative as suggested by the physicist David Bohm (along with his writing sidekick, David Peat) in the book *Science, Order, and Creativity*, is to watch overstating your intellectual points as such points are often tentative.

James Flynn (and some less noted earlier researchers) noticed that IQ scores in many countries appeared to be rising during the twentieth century [Pinker 2011; Folger]. Although there is plenty controversy here, the apparent rising IQ's appear to be accepted. The "bombshell" as Pinker put it "is that the Flynn effect is almost certainly environmental" [Pinker 2011, p.653]. How such an environmental dynamic could have been missed in other studies - and also everyday perception - of intelligence is truly amazing, though.

Steven Pinker points out that:

> [c]ould the world be getting not just more literate and knowledgeable but actually smarter? Might people be increasingly adept at learning new skills, grasping abstract ideas, and solving unfore-

seen problems? Amazingly, the answer is yes. Intelligence Quotient (IQ) scores have been rising for more than a century, in every part of the world, at a rate of about three IQ points (a fifth of a standard deviation) per decade [Pinker 2018, p.240].

This finding is amazing but perhaps like the abilities of prodigies it might best be categorized as a mystery. The evidence for the climbing scores is strong and it is only its source that is controversial. Pinker not surprisingly dismisses a DNA basis - we have "not engaged in a massive eugenics project" (and moreover the DNA basis for the variation in intelligence is still missing) - but suggests that the key has been improvements in education, in particular ones which have somehow boosted our analytic mindset. While the more concrete educational topics like general knowledge have risen a little bit on IQ tests, it has been with the more subtle topic of analytic reasoning that the big gains have been realized.

Pinker suggests that improved nutrition and health may well have made some contributions but that the key was again improved education. That nutrition claim was put to test in a recent article assessing the impact of contemporary nutrition in which it was suggested that, "[p]oor diet is the leading cause of mortality in the United States" [Mozaffarian and Glickman]. The article provided associated national estimates for the economic costs of heart disease and diabetes (both over 300 billion per year) and also obesity which is estimated at "1.72 trillion per year, or 9.3 percent of gross domestic product". I find it difficult to believe that these dietary trends are simultaneously boosting our IQs.

The observed historical gains in intelligence are truly remarkable. I borrow from Pinker's fuller descriptions in his *The Better Angels of Our Nature* where he wrote that:

> [a]n average teenager today, if he or she could time-travel back to 1950, would have an IQ of 118. If the teenager went back to 1910, he or she would have had an IQ of 130, besting 98 percent of his or her contemporaries. Yes, you [read] that right: if we take the Flynn Effect at face value, a typical person today is smarter than 98 percent of the people in the good old days of 1910. To state it in an even more jarring way, a typical person of 1910, if time-transported forward to the present, would have a mean IQ of 70, which is at the border of mental retardation. With the Raven's Progressive Matrices, a test that is sometimes considered the purest measure of general intelligence, the rise is even steeper. An ordinary person of 1910 would have an IQ of

50 today, which is smack in the middle of mentally retarded territory, between "moderate" and "mild" retardation [Pinker 2011, p.651].

Flynn himself feels that these increases in IQ scores reflect a pervasive shift in modern societies towards an increasing focus on abstract reasoning [Flynn; Pinker 2011, pp.653-54; Folger]. Flynn hypothesized that this shift involved "scientific reasoning" infiltrating "everyday thinking" on an increasingly wide scale [Flynn; Pinker 2011, p.655]. Steven Pinker offered an explanation that many modern people have apparently "assimilated hundreds of these [scientific] abstractions from casual reading, conversation, and exposure to the media, including *proportional, percentage, correlation, causation, control group, placebo, representative sample, false positive, empirical, post hoc, statistical, median, variability, circular argument, tradeoff,* and *cost-benefit analysis*" [Pinker 2011, p.655]. This may be true in a few places like Cambridge, Massachusetts, but I doubt it is accurate elsewhere. With such a hypothesized shift towards abstraction, Flynn suggested that "we developed new cognitive skills and the kind of brain that can deal with them" [Flynn].

While the evidence for this rising innate analytical reasoning capacity again appears to be strong, I think that the evidence for its educational cause is not, and furthermore that the resulting realized boost in an everyday sense certainly is not. Nothing that I have seen during my lifetime suggests that the average demonstrated intelligence (versus potential intelligence) is rising. In fact from my conversations with professors; from critical readings from the academic achievement front; and from teachers' comments in the *New York Times*; these together suggest that there has been a decline. I suggest the big driver behind this decline in our actual smarts has been the rising presence of electronic-based distraction and secondarily decreases in physical activity [Raichlen and Alexander].

A simple counterexample to the claim that people are getting "actually smarter" appeared in a group of Flynn effect-related articles published by the *New York Times*. In it the intelligence researcher Linda Gottfredson's pointed out complexity barriers apparent in a 1993 literacy survey amongst American adults [Gottfredson]. Some results included that only about 17 percent were able to use "a bus schedule to determine the appropriate bus for a given set of conditions" and only 3 percent were capable of answering "the most complex questions, like determining the total cost of carpet to cover a room (using a calculator)". These elite subsets were also capable of handling simpler tasks such as finding a specified piece of information in a sports article and also filling in some given information into an auto maintenance record. Additionally, I doubt that such test results would be better now given our further slide into distraction.

Another contrary example can be found in Walter Williams' article "Higher Education in America". Williams' cited the following information from Richard Arum and Josipa Roksa's *Academically Adrift: Limited Learning on College Campuses*:

> after surveying 2,300 students at various college, argues that very little improvement in critical reasoning skills occurs in college. Adult literacy is falling among college graduates. Large portions of college graduates do not know simple facts, such as the half-century in which the Civil War occurred. There are exceptions to this academic incompetency, most notably in technical areas such as engineering, nursing, architecture and accounting, where colleges teach vocationally useful material [Williams Higher Ed].

Williams also cites the recent book *Restoring the Promise: Higher Education in America* by Richard K. Vedder. Williams included the following derived from Vedder's book:

> student ineptitude is not surprising since they spend little time in classrooms and studying. It's even less surprising when one considers student school preparation. According to 2010 and 2013 NAEP test score, only 37% of 12th-graders were proficient in reading, 25% in math, 12% in history, 20% in geography and 24% in civics.

This of course significant and again furthers my sense that the rising IQ phenomena might better be viewed as a mystery (along with others mysteries including prodigies).

Chapter 4 - Not Awakening: Sam Harris and Scientific Buddhism

This chapter's essay focuses on Sam Harris' book, *Waking Up*, as well as the associated contemporary makeover of the traditional religion of Buddhism. Harris nominally attempts to strip out the "metaphysical ideas ... [of] ignorant and isolated people of the past" [Harris, p.33] and thus offer a science-kosher guide to studying your own consciousness via meditation, with a particular aim of "self-transcendence" or enlightenment. His work and also my rebuttal here are significantly based on personal experiences. This chapter is indirectly a commentary on the contemporary hegemony of science. It touches on some issues, though, that could be of general interest.

This chapter is inherently loose as it attempts to weave together a sober depiction of meditational practice against the loose claims of *Waking Up*. As a succinct introductory synopsis, Harris misses many essentials. The secularization/science-ification push of the book was neither novel nor necessary. In the West, Buddhist practice has for decades been pushed in a largely areligious fashion with significant overlapping efforts to tie the practice to science and moreover an intellectual perspective. Furthermore, significant enlightenment experiences are very rare and thus the rigors of traditional monastic practice. If Harris' points about the efficacy of meditation (and also drugs) for personal transformation were valid then they should be self-evident given the cumulative extent of involvement with both in the West. Finally, the scientific certainty on which he builds his arguments did not exist when he wrote the book or obviously now.

A. A General Discussion on Waking Up

To get this chapter started I provide some of my own relevant background. I have been involved with daily meditational and Buddhist's practices for over 40 years. I am not a philosophically inclined person. My ongoing interests in dealing with the challenges of life (for myself and others) has reinforced that seemingly innate tendency. I am also not bewitched by science and moreover have a strong tendency to be bothered by hubris and the pursuit of cleverness.

Near the end of the book Sam Harris' states the objective of *Waking Up*:

> [u]ntil we can talk about spirituality in rational terms - acknowledging the validity of self-transcendence - our world will remain shattered by dogmatism. This book has been my attempt to begin such a conversation [p.203].

This framing quote is a good place to begin an expose on the nonsense going on in *Waking Up*. First off, dogmatism is symptomatic of human rigidity and it is omni-present and regularly divisive. One of the appealing messages coming out of scientism is that you can simply shun religion and embrace (or simply nod your head to) science and you are good to go in a largely unencumbered intellectual sense. Remember religion supposedly ruins everything and followers of science are supposedly freethinkers (despite the lack of scientific support for the requisite existence of free will). In fact as a human being you can get rigidly hung up anywhere. As a simple gross example, consider the super-rigid nature of political discourse.

At no point in his book does Harris acknowledge the work of the neurologist and longtime Zen practitioner, James H. Austin. Austin has written a series of books trying to make neural sense out of Zen (Buddhist) practice including his own enlightenment experience (apparently an introductory or kensho experience). His writings are extensive and coincidentally like Vaclav Smil they were published via MIT Press. Amongst the wide range of topics in his first book, *Zen and the Brain: Toward an Understanding of Meditation and Consciousness*, Austin included a critical look at drug experiences [Austin]. In total, as of my earlier page-counting effort it appears that James Austin had published 2,140 pages predating *Waking Up*'s publication.

Well somehow you might excuse Harris for omitting this earlier extensive work, after all James Austin was not (and I assume still is not) on the celebrity author circuit. But this apparent oversight is the tip of the iceberg-sized problem here. At no point in my previous scouring of Austin's writings have I seen evidence that Austin even acknowledged the underlying metaphysical/religious framework (specifically life-after-life) of Buddhist's practice (which of course includes Zen). But for someone who has followed the Western Buddhist - or really for the most part, Buddhist-derivative - contemporary scene, Austin's oversight was not surprising. For as long as I have been involved with Buddhist practice the overwhelming tendency has been to pretend around its religious beliefs and framework. Thus Buddhism in the West did not need Harris to introduce the conversation because the scienc-ification and/or secularization tendency has largely been the default process for decades. In a physical sense it appears that most involved Westerners have treated the marginally incorporated religious aspects of Buddhism like people in general treat gift wrapping. You pull it off, throw it out (or in the gift case, attempt to recycle it), and then forget it.

I introduce another point from Austin's work before moving on. James Austin was strongly motivated by a big objective question - how is it that a short term internal experience can seemingly have longterm positive consequences? From a materialist perspective that is the sixty four thousand dollar question surrounding enlightenment. Somehow such brief experiences appear capable of engendering significant positive psyche changes. For historical evidence here I would suggest that the very long record of serious meditational efforts in part reflects this phenomenon. People have observed such changes in others and pursue meditation hoping for their own transformations. Austin opened his *Zen and the Brain* with his "straightforward thesis" that "[deep] awakening, enlightenment occurs only because the human brain undergoes substantial changes" which were suggested to "both profoundly enhance yet simplify, the working of the brain [Austin, p.xix]. Austin's book stepped up to the materialist plate and attempted to provide a brain-based answer which was the neural thing to do, although clearly not an easy thing. The brain, like the rest of the body, is susceptible to transient events inflicting serious setbacks, but the plausibility of short term lasting enhancement is difficult to comprehend. Sam Harris's book should certainly have addressed this question but it didn't.

I will hit pause here on Harris' supposed conversation-starting. For some relevant context on Buddhism and meditation I present some points from the academics, Robert E. Buswell, Jr. and Donald S. Lopez, Jr., in their article "10 Misconceptions about Buddhism" [Buswell and Lopez]. The first of their misconceptions is that "All Buddhists meditate" which the authors rebutted in part with "[m]editation has traditionally been considered a monastic practice, and even then, a speciality only of certain monks". The effectiveness of meditation tends to be grossly overstated in the West and Harris stays consistent with this. With his suggested ease of enlightenment experiences, including the questionable validity of his own, Harris appears to be off the mark.

Buswell and Lopez's next three misconceptions were relatively minor - "[t]he primary form of Buddhist meditation is mindfulness", all "Buddhists are vegetarians", and all "Buddhists are pacifists". The fifth misconception was a big one, though, "Buddhism is a philosophy and not a religion". In its entirety this entry read:

> Buddhism has many philosophical schools, with a sophistication equal to that of any philosophical school that developed in Europe. However, Buddhism is a religion, by any definition of that indefinable term, unless one defines religion as a belief in a creator God. The great majority of Buddhist practice over history, for both monks and laypeople, has been focused on a good rebirth in the next lifetime, whether for oneself, one's family, or for all beings in the universe.

This is arguably the central misconception about Buddhism as it is interpreted by most Western practitioners and Harris should have stated this. The religious framework of Buddhism was likely inherited in part from the common premodern life-after-life vision. Buddhist practices - including meditational ones - were apparently designed to help people better deal with the challenges and vicissitudes of serial lives.

A point repeatedly made by Sam Harris is the unlikeliness if not absurdity of any such dualistic vision, and moreover who would want or need context beyond this life anyway? Harris at one point, in a relatively polite way, suggested that:

> whatever happens after death, it is possible to justify a life of spiritual practice and self-transcendence without pretending to know things we do not know [p.186].

It is also possible to justify trying to make sense of an understanding of life that beget a practice you find critically important. Harris' revered teacher was called Tulku Urgyen Rinpoche. "Rinpoche" translates as teacher and "tulku" translates as incarnate. The latter implying that he was selected as a young child, by "ignorant and isolated" people, as being the reincarnation of a formerly accomplished meditation practitioner (and coincidentally he apparently filled those shoes pretty well). I also point out that the suggestion to not pretend "to know things that we do not know" could well be applied to Harris' allegiance to the assumptions of science which led him to chuckle off as "pure delusion"; "simply ignorant about the nature of living systems"; and as "wholly imaginary" any basis for questioning materialism.

The most fundamental point I am making in this book is that the sacred DNA-based understanding of life is getting clobbered and that one way or another people should start looking elsewhere for explanations. That clobbering was underway at least 5 years before *Waking Up* was written. The issue is more than philosophical, it is also practical. Readers can look up the expected DNA-disease connections within personal genomics and note their significance. If faulty DNA did not stack the deck in favor of a person's difficult condition(s), then what did?

Continuing with Buswell and Lopez's tour of misconceptions, the sixth misconception was, "[t]he Buddha was a human being, not a god, and the religion he founded has no place for the worship of gods". This is perhaps where Sam Harris *et al* would like it. Here Buswell and Lopez's entry was:

> Buddhism has an elaborate pantheon of celestial beings (devas, etymologically related to the English word "divinity") and advanced spiritual beings (bodhisattvas and buddhas), who occupy various heavens and pure lands and who respond to the prayers of the devout.

Next, on the presumed anti-religious form of Buddhism, Zen, the authors had an entry titled, "Zen rejects conventional Buddhism. Zen masters burn statues of the Buddha, scorn the sutras [teaching of the Buddha], and regularly frequent bars and brothels". Harris makes a few derogatory comments about Zen but missed its minimalistic appeal. If you want science-kosher/this-life-only oriented practice, then Zen - at least as it has been practiced in the West (and followed by people like James Austin) - appears quite optimal. Here the entry was:

> Zen monks follow a strict set of regulations, called "pure rules," which are based on the monastic discipline imported from India. Most Zen monks have engaged in extensive study of Buddhist scriptures before beginning their training in the meditation hall. And although one of the Four Phrases of Zen is "not relying on words and letters," Zen has the largest body of written literature of any tradition within East Asian Buddhism.

Another basic point neglected in Harris' book is that morality or discipline tends to be a vital contributor to the potential helpfulness of meditational practices. The "quality of one's mind" and with it one's meditation practice is significantly influenced by the quality of one's actions. This basic point about discipline or morality should be evident to any adult, and even more apparent to those who meditate regularly. Another basic point of Buddhist practice is to try to build a helpful or compassionate inclination towards other beings. This might be dismissed as simply being nice ethical posturing but its purpose is said to be transformative. The desired inclination is usually termed bodhicitta and it is often characterized as essential to the possibility of signifiant enlightenment transformations. This is routinely mentioned in Tibetan literature, see for example Lama Yeshe's fine *Introduction to Tantra: The Transformation of Desire*.

The ninth misconception also happened to be dedicated to Zen and in its entirety was (with the opening line here being the title-misconception):

> Zen is dedicated to the experience of "sudden enlightenment," which frees its followers from the extended regimens of training in ethics, meditation, and wisdom found in conventional forms of Buddhism. Zen monks routinely expect to spend decades in full-time practice before they will be able to make real progress in their meditation.

The last point here is a rebut to the very prevalent contemporary fantasies with regards to the ease of meditational progress and thus the likeliness of Harris' goal in *Waking Up*.

Harris' should have provided an example of a meditation-based enlightenment experience. This is the central focus of his book and such experiences are quite unique. Here I provide an example of an enlightenment (or Self-realization) account as given in a modern introduction to Zen practice, *The Three Pillars of Zen* [Kapleau, pp.215-219]. The following excerpts were written by a Japanese executive in the 1950's. In an initial note to his Zen teacher the executive had written:

> You remember the discussion which arose about Self-realization centering around that American. At that time I hardly imagined that in a few days I would be reporting to you my own experience.

The executive went on to describe that during the train ride home from the monastery with his wife he had been deeply struck whilst reading a passage from Zen literature. The particular passage read was "I came to realize clearly that Mind is no other than mountains and rivers and the great wide earth, the sun and the moon and the stars".

This passage somehow deeply resonated with this man and his meditational experiences. During the subsequent days it triggered an enlightenment experience (in the awkward company of his family and brother and sister-in-law). During his first night home he wrote that:

> [a]t midnight I abruptly awakened. At first my mind was foggy, then suddenly that quotation flashed into my consciousness: "I came to realize that Mind is no other than mountains, rivers, and the great wide earth, the sun and the moon and the stars". And I repeated it. Then all at once I was struck as though by lightening, and the next instant heaven and earth crumbled and disappeared. Instantly, like surging waves, a tremendous delight welled up in me, a veritable hurricane of delight, as I laughed wildly and loudly: "Ha, ha, ha, ha, ha, ha! There's no reasoning here, no reasoning at all! Ha, ha, ha!" The empty sky split in two, then opened its mouth and began to laugh uproariously: "Ha, ha, ha!".

The executive then went on to exclaim, "I've come to enlightenment! Shakyamuni [i.e., the Buddha] and the patriarchs have not deceived me!" This revelatory experience then got a bit awkward as his family was clueless about his inner experiences so the executive downshifted and apologized for his outbursts.

The next day the executive went to visit a Zen teacher and he was simply overcome with joy and wept. That teacher reportedly commented, "it is rare indeed to experience to such a wonderful degree. It is termed 'Attainment of the emptiness of Mind'. You are to be congratulated." As a possible crude explanation here, somehow his extensive meditation practice plus the triggering of the quote allowed him to vividly break through the deeply-entrenched, me-and-the-world story that we operate within.

His enlightenment breakthrough continued across the next few days and left him "laughing and weeping" extensively. The executive then contacted his original teacher in hopes of offering some inspiration to his monks and also in hopes of helping the novice American. To the latter he suggested letting him know that "even I, who am unworthy and lacking in spirit, can grasp such a wonderful experience when time matures". He further suggested telling that American - who not surprisingly was hoping for enlightenment within a week - that, "don't say days, weeks, or even lifetimes.

Don't say millions of billions of kalpa. Tell him to vow to attain enlightenment though it takes the infinite, the boundless, the incalculable future". A kalpa is an extremely long period of time.

The executive's subsequent diary entries included, "Am totally at peace at peace at peace", "Am supremely free free free free free", and "The substance of Mind - this is now luminously clear to me". And finally in a concluding paragraph he wrote that:

> The ancients said the enlightened mind is comparable to a fish swimming. That's exactly how it is - there's no stagnation. I feel no hinderance. Everything flows smoothly, freely. Everything goes naturally. This limitless freedom is beyond all expression. What a wonderful world.

The executive finally stated simply, "I am grateful, so grateful."

Of some note here is that an enlightenment experience like the above is simply not on the radar screen of someone like Steven Pinker or more generally science. Pinker's perspective on "enlightenment" is simply an intellectual one. Along those lines, years ago in talking with a highly educated physicist they simply categorized such revelations as episodes of schizophrenia or craziness. They certainly don't make equation-sense. To Harris' credit, though, his book is trying to legitimatize such experiences which have a long history of occurrences in meditational and mystical traditions.

On the other hand, Harris tends to lock enlightenment experiences into a somewhat superficial "self-transcendence" description, involving ending your identification with thought. Some of the most lucid descriptions of the enlightened state (and moreover meditation) that I have encountered are in the remarkable conversations with the Indian Advaita Vedanta teacher, Sri Nisargadatta Maharaj. His big book is affirmatively titled *I AM THAT* [Nisagadatta] and it attempts to convey the nature of subjective reality (including a super-self or Self) when it is decoupled from the default me-and-the-world story. One of Nisagadatta's basic points is that once you can clearly observe the me-business at work (and see that you are *NOT THAT*) that perception opens the door to a deeper experience of life and self (and you are *THAT*). That experience is apparently enlightenment. In one succinct exchange with a student Nisargadatta suggests that by reigning in excessive imagination and attachment we are then simply able to "see [reality] as it is, not through the screen of desire and fear" [Nisargadatta, p.286]

Additionally, an important point here is that significant experiences (like the previous executive's) are rare and almost inevitably come from long dedicated practice. Harris claims that the Dzogchen teacher he visited, Tulko Urgyen Rinpoche, matter of factly brought him to enlightenment and moreover could do so for others. If anything like this was true then Harris' description of that experience would likely be considerably more profound; there would have been a mile-long line at Tulku Urgyen's door; and the actual training associated with (the Tibetan Buddhist) Dzogchen practice would not be such a long, rigorous, and largely a monastic affair. This tendency to trivialize Dzogchen training to Westerners in fact got one of Sam Harris' former teachers, Lama Surya Das (a Westerner), denounced by his own Tibetan teacher.

As an aside for more serious consideration, some readers might want to read an online interview with Tulku Urgyen Rinpoche [Kunsang]. That interview conveys the very serious nature of Dzogchen training - pitfalls and all. I think a basic point here is that some teachers of Tibetan Buddhism, and certainly their Western followers, have under-appreciated the extensive practice traditionally expected prior to an unstructured teaching like the Dzogchen's highest form. In the above sited interview Tulky Urgyen mentions that as part of his own background he did some training involving "reciting the Mani". Reciting that mantra (Om Mani Padme Hum) in simplest terms is supposed to help the practitioner develop a very unified or focused mind state. In that sense it is sort of word-directed (and sometimes image-assisted) focused mindfulness exercise. In any case Tulku Urgyen did that all day long as part of his preliminary training. And he did this for 3 years! Such monastic dedication might have been pretty common in traditional Tibet, but that is not the case in the contemporary Western world.

Continuing with the enlightenment commentary, I have been around some serious practitioners, including of course monastic figures, my sense is that such transformations really are profound and can having lasting impacts. In very simple physical terms it is as though the default condition as human beings were to walk around with pebbles in our shoes. Enlightenment in that simple analogy is when a person finds a way to shed those pebbles. Thus, you can sense in others that via a significant enlightenment experience they are considerably more at ease with themselves and life. Another physical analogy would be that they learn to ride a bicycle, not an ordinary bicycle, but the bike of life. The bike riding analogy is appropriate here in that it is *not* an intellectual development. It is a big deal and that transformation can indirectly motivate others to try to meditate.

I add two more references here of potential interest to some readers. The first is of an even deeper enlightenment experience that also happened in Japan. That experience happened to a very sick young Japanese woman, Yaeko Iwasaki, in the 1930's and is also described in Kapleau's *The Three Pillars of Zen* (Chapter 6 and is also available online at [Iwasaki/Kapleau]). The inherent sense of responsibility, humility, and deeper perspective on life and death suggested through this experience are noteworthy. Additionally, after marching through a sequence of breakthroughs in only a week Iwasaki came to realize the significance of deep enlightenment experiences and accept her pending death (which she could sense coming). Finally, the fact that this happened to a lay person is very remarkable.

A second reference that might be of interest for additional reading is the story of a Japanese man, Ittetsu Nemoto, who plunged into traditional (and barely still existent) monastic Rinzai Zen training and then subsequently dedicated himself to helping out with suicide prevention efforts in Japan. A fine article, *The Last Call*, describing this was published in the *New Yorker* magazine and was written by Larissa MacFarquhar [MacFarquhar]. Nemoto's journey is remarkable for a number of reasons. He managed in his intense journey to stay clear of two meditational tendencies - the first is too much withdrawal (admittedly this option has faded a lot) and secondly his apparent complete lack of interest in intellectualizing (Nemoto is no Sam Harris). But MacFarquhar's article nicely portrays Nemoto's extremely rigorous training; seemingly miraculous Self-realization experience (apparently an initial or Kensho experience); serious dedication to helping in the outside world; and his sober conclusion that we learn and are potentially transformed through suffering - and likely intense suffering at that. That last point seems to be unpopular in general and probably less so amongst intellectuals.

Here I will attempt to further convey the unlikeliness of significant enlightenment experiences which Harris' even went so far as attributing to drug usage. I indirectly get started with an observation of myself. Set against a number of challenges I have faced in my life there seems to be one mundane constant. That is no matter how derailed I can get in some areas in a basic objective 2 + 2 = 4 sense I tend to stay grounded. That same nerd tendency has surfaced itself for years within the Western Buddhist scene where the availability of enlightenment experiences are greatly oversold. An additional important point I will return to, is the minimally discussed, potential instability of such transformations in the lay world.

From a seemingly parallel perspective I note that a Western meditation teacher, A. H. Almaas, had written:

> [a] realized teacher might have thousands of students but it is rare if even a handful of them actually attain liberation [Almaas p.4].

A. H. Almaas had been a physics graduate student when he decided to exit that scientific pursuit and instead apply himself to meditative inquiry. Also the notable and neglected physicist David Bohm, after spending years in sort of a part-time, super-intellectual sidekick role to the meditation-oriented philosopher Jiddu Krishnamurti, made the same point about the rarity of significant enlightenment experiences and suggested this rarity as a historical tendency [Bohm and Peat]. This makes sense.

Another very well-grounded assessment of the likelihood of enlightenment was given at the end of the Zen classic, *Zen Teaching of Huang Po*, by John Blofeld [Blofeld]. In it the famous Zen teacher Huang Po commented that:

> Ah be diligent. Be diligent! Of a thousand or ten thousand attempting to enter by this [Zen enlightenment] Gate, only three or perhaps five pass through. If you are heedless of my warnings, calamity is sure to follow. Therefore it is written, "Exert your strength in THIS life to attain! Or else incur long aeons of further [karmic] gain!" [p.132].

Even in a much less distraction-prone era, a practice very much focused on this life, in a likely super-rigorous Zen monastery saw limited success. By comparison, how many modern Western meditational outfits - nominally Buddhist or otherwise - do not grossly oversell the return on meditation and with it the availability of enlightenment?

As a followup point here, Huang Po is coming from the traditional Zen (actually in China, Chan) perspective. In it you want to very seriously pursue having a deep enlightenment experience so that you can immediately end your gross dissatisfaction with life. That experience is also supposed to free up an individual from the compulsions or cravings which in the future could lead to rebirth. This latter goal does seem to conflict, though, with the oft-stated religious commitment of helping others in the future (as is commonly chanted in the Bodhisattva Vows) and thus returning to help out. In comparison most other forms of Buddhist practice are more modest than Chan/Zen in their ambitions and use simple practices to try to stabilize and improve your life and also - and this is the religious part - your post-death trajectory and even possibly facilitating an enlightenment breakthrough in the disembodied or intermediate state. Whereas Huang Po expresses dismay over the possibility of reincarnating, others in Buddhism (certainly many Mahayana Buddhists) appear committed to coming back to help out and also potentially learning some more lessons.

I add a related parallel point. Years ago when I regularly attended meetings for an anti-(or really reduced)-nuclear weapons group there was another attendee that drew my attention. That attendee was an older man who seemed remarkably at ease with life and himself. Eventually I spoke to the man after one of the meetings and asked him about his background. With my own background (and biases) I assumed he must have been involved with meditation (and probably for years at that). But that was not the case. The man reported that he had been involved with a small Christian church. Perhaps similarly, the book *And There Was Light* by Jacque Lusseyran reports on the jaw-dropping achievements of a group of young people in the French resistance [Lusseyran]. Lusseyran, and apparently some of his other very brave and deeply insightful colleagues, seemed to have been Christians via their own understanding. Whatever the vehicle, though, such mystical or religious transformations appear to be rare. A general positive point, though, is that based on my personal observations I think some people can find real benefit (and with it, be quite beneficial) as a result of their religious efforts (even if they don't come close a profound transformation).

I go on to add here that I do not think that Sam Harris' presentation of enlightenment is accurate. His teacher-facilitated awakening in fact sounds similar to the woman's awakening that he playfully critiqued in his book. He should have mentioned that there is enormous pressure on teachers to convey some sense of success to students if only so that the latter will stick around. If awakenings were as commonly available as Harris suggests then we should know this. Largely secular Buddhist meditational practices have been pretty widely available for at least 4 decades now, it should be commonly known that people can find some very helpful psyche shifts via meditating. The same situation could be said of drug usage. From my own observations I think that meditation can be helpful in simple sustained ways, starting with being an attention-encouraging habit. Additionally, from what

I have seen being around drug users I wouldn't even endorse a net helpful there (benefits for some conditions has garnered positive media but I suggest waiting several more years). Net effects are what matters and if you can get net positives that is great. The sober nature of life seems to be reflected in that fact that most net positives consist of simply avoiding harmful activities.

After an initial promise to avoid attacks on religions and the religious, Harris drifts back to that habit in *Waking Up*. Thus a person who states that meditation helps make "it impossible to stay angry for more than a few moments" and further that it allows you to "discover that negative states of mind vanish all by themselves" continues with his part-time career of sniping at the religious. I suggest that if Harris were truly "intellectually honest" he would find plenty of reason to question the scientific regime, perhaps beginning with his own profession of neuroscience. He might do this simply to try to balance his perspective with regards to the charged Religion-versus-Science standoff.

In the period in which Harris was writing there were thankfully a number of neuroscientists who wrote publicly about the big gap between the common hype and the actual state of neuroscience. A prominent example was the previously introduced, Rafael Yuste and George M. Church's *Scientific American* article with the overly-optimistic title, "The New Century of the Brain: Big Science lights the way to an understanding of how the world's most complex machine gives rise to our thoughts and emotions" [Yuste and Church]. That article offers a substantial introduction to the very big technical developments and subsequent longterm efforts that appear necessary for neuroscience to really grasp brain functioning (if materialism holds true). Yuste and Church thus suggested that what is needed is:

> a new set of technologies that will enable investigators to monitor and also alter the electrical activity of thousands or even millions of neurons - techniques capable of deciphering what the Spanish neuroanatomist Santiago Ramon y Cajal called the impenetrable jungles were many investigators have lost themselves.

That article also undercuts the faith that Harris exhibits with regards to the accuracy or validity of neural imaging studies.

Harris states that:

> [t]here is now a large literature on the psychological benefits of meditation. Different techniques produce long-lasting changes in attention, emotion, cognition, and pain perception, and these correlate with both structural and functional changes in the brain. This field of research is quickly growing, as is our understanding of self-awareness and related phenomena. Given recent advances in neuroimaging technology, we no longer face a practical impediment to investigating spiritual insights in the context of science [Harris, p.8].

If these were true they should be readily apparent in person and thus likely be common knowledge. From my observations "long-lasting changes" in a deep positive sense are not easy and thus tend to be rare, and this probably reflects the rarity of significant enlightenment or analogous transformation experiences, as well as the ongoing demands of life. The meditation practice historically had a special home in monasteries and probably in large part this was to facilitate transformations and then help stabilize them (analogous reasoning and efforts may have of course been found in other forms of monasteries too). On the latter point readers might note how the previously mentioned Ittetsu Nemoto (of "The Last Call") ultimately struggled when he returned to lay life and then eventually turned back towards a monastery-based existence (although he continued to offer help along the suicide prevention front).

Roughly concurrent with Harris' claims was a November 2014 *Scientific American* article, "mind of the meditator", by Mathieu Ricard, Antoine Lutz, and Richard J. Davidson [Richard *et al*]. That neural-meditation article mentioned the associated inspirational efforts of the Dalai Lama. It considered neural imaging changes apparently associated with three meditational techniques categorized as mindfulness, focused attention, and compassion and loving kindness. The authors made some Harris-like clams with regards to the efficacy of meditation including:

> [a]bout 15 years of research have done more than show that meditation produces significant changes in both the function and structure of the brains of experienced practitioners. These studies are now starting to demonstrate that contemplative practices may have a substantive impact on biological processes critical for physical health.

Of note here is that "experienced practitioners" implies people with over 10,000 hours of meditation experience. At a rate of an hour a day that translates to over 27 years of practicing meditation. The article further stated that:

> [t]he ability to cultivate compassion and other positive qualities lays the foundation for an ethical framework unattached to any philosophy or religion, which could have a profoundly beneficial effect on all aspects of human societies.

Again I suggest this is analogous to the message of *Waking Up* and it also is too optimistic. The meditator's mind article seems loosely quantitative and the one graph which purports to show enhancement in neural features derived from meditation shows small effects with significant overlap between the measurements of experienced meditators and those of controls. The authors also failed to respond to a published follow-up letter from a meditator regarding the possibility that their results could have been distorted by selection bias. How many lay people have a chance of joining the 10,000 hour club (and thus the possibility of selection bias)?

More seriously, though, why can't Sam Harris and Mathieu Ricard *et al* acknowledge that secularly-packaged meditation has been quite widely available in the West for at least 40 years? If such meditation was as self-help productive as presented in Richard *et al*'s article and Harris' *Waking Up*, then why didn't it sell itself - like an effective dieting routine would have - without the need for neuro-scientific promotion? I mentioned that to an older very experienced American meditator and she simply nodded her head in agreement. Five years down the road from these publications, other than the apparent growth in possibly trendy mindfulness programs and mindfulness-oriented magazines, I haven't seen evidence of a wave of transformation.

Furthermore, I suggest the sober contemporary question here is - has the mindfulness *et al* self-help oriented movement even dented the formidable dis-attention tsunami underway in our society via electronics? That context was not even mentioned in *Waking Up* (or in Ricard *et al*'s article). I think if it were possible to regulate cellphones in such a way as to reduce their usage by a factor of two, that would likely do more to help society's state of mindfulness than the official mindfulness movement. Gross dis-attention appears to be an enormous problem. I add here that I think of screen-time as tending to be the opposite of meditation-time.

Sam Harris confidently presents his split brain experiment-based argument for a brain-only vision of our mind or self. He points out such patients appears to have two selves and thus our sense of a unified self (and thus possibly soul) is a neural-concocted illusion. But he doesn't mention any simple counterarguments. First, in an everyday sense we can all experience the presence of apparent multiple selves when experiencing our competing desires. Additionally, in a neural sense the earlier mentioned work of John Lorber provides easy counterexamples [Lewin]. When there is good evidence that people can function normally - and even have a high IQ - but have gross deficiencies in neural volume that challenges the basic assumptions of neuroscience. With roughly 5 percent normal brain volume how do you neurally argue for a normal sense of self, let alone the possibility of fragmenting it into two or more selves?

Additionally, in Lorber's work the symmetry assumption that Harris (and neuroscience in general) utilize was also challenged. Lorber looked at patients in which the offending ventricle expansion was limited to one side of the brain. Thus such patients should have seen limitations associated with the compromise of that hemisphere. But as Lorber observed:

> I've now seen more than 50 cases of [such] asymmetrical hydrocephalus and the interesting thing is that only a minority of these individuals show the expected and long-cherished neurological finding of paralysis with spasticity on the opposite side of the body.

Lorber then went on to point out that one of these patients displayed spastic paralysis on the *same* side as their "enormously enlarged ventricles". Why haven't such findings found their way into neuroscience coverage? Note you might substitute the expected "spastic paralysis" into Harris' hypothesized hemispheric-based, dual self argument. The marked damaging or removal of a hemisphere's volume should produce significant limitations on the opposite side of the body's functioning, but that is not what was observed in a number of cases.

Harris' point with his arguments here is of course to rebut the possibility of dualistic, and thus possibly religious, perspectives. Other basic unacknowledged challenges to his point include the aforementioned innate religious perspectives described in the book *Born Believers* by Justin Barrett. How in a molecular-only sense do you explain the existence of such innate beliefs? But a more direct brain-oriented challenge could be in the phenomena of terminal lucidity. That phenomenon is discussed in a *Scientific*

American blog piece by Jesse Bering entitled, "One Last Goodbye/ The Strange Case of Terminal Lucidity" [Bering 2014]. In his writeup Bering considers something that was possibly first officially characterized by a German biologist Michael Nahm in a 2009 article. Nahm described terminal lucidity as:

> The (re-)emergence of normal or unusually enhanced mental abilities in dull, unconscious, or mentally ill patients shortly before death, including considerable elevation of mood and spiritual affectation, or the ability to speak in a previously unusual spiritualized and elated manner.

In a subsequent Nahm article, written along with Bruce Greyson, it was mentioned that in a study of 49 cases, 41 of the cases involved surprising verbalizations occurring during the last week of life. Furthermore, in 21 of the cases the verbalizations came on the same day as death. In some cases severely limited individuals have gradually returned to near normal lucidity before their deaths. One case involved a man who had been completely catatonic for nearly 2 decades before his reemergence to a near normal state.

The other cases involved sudden lucidity. In one case Bering reported that a 92 year old woman "with advanced Alzheimer's disease, …, hadn't recognized her family for years, but the day before her death, she had a pleasant bright conversation with them, recalling everyone's name … [and] was even aware of her age and where she'd been living all this time". But the most striking case involved a severely disabled young woman named Anna ("Kathe") Katherina Ehmer and it occurred in 1922. Her case had substantial verification in that as a patient in a mental hospital or asylum her sudden lucidity episode was observed by the asylum's chief physician Wilhem Wittneben and also its director Friedrich Happich. The two men independently and apparently consistently (reportedly "[o]ver the years") communicated Kathe's remarkable spontaneous event. Kathe had been severely disabled and Happich described her as having been from birth on:

> seriously retarded. She had never learned to speak a single word. She stared for hours on a particular spot, then fidgeted for hours without a break. She gorged her food, fouled herself day and night, uttered an animal-like sound, and slept … never taking notice of her environment even for a second.

She also apparently had suffered a number of bouts of severe meningitis infections which were believed to have damaged her cortical brain tissue.

She also experienced a bout of tuberculosis which led to the amputation of a leg.

Shortly after the removal of her leg Kathe was laying in bed and was approaching death. At this point a number of staff members, including Wittneben and Happich, gathered to observe her stunning rejuvenation. As Happich described it:

> Kathe who had never spoken a single word, being entirely mentally disabled from birth on, sang dying songs to herself. Specifically, she sang over and over again, *"Where does the soul find its home, its peace? Peace, peace, heavenly peace!"* For half an hour she sang. Her face, up to then so stultified, was transfigured and spiritualized. Then she quietly passed away.

So what can you do with this from the materialist perspective? Has someone in neuroscience ever acknowledged the challenge imposed by such phenomena? To his credit Jesse Bering - with a job in psychology and at one point a blog at *Scientific American* - can write in super-understated fashion that, "on face value, one has to admit that the story of Kathe Ehmer is something of a puzzle".

Bering had some personal motivation in this matter, though, since he had been with his dying mother who had managed "five minutes of perfect communion with me when, ostensibly, all her cognitive functions were already lost". If Sam Harris really wants to make his case against dualism then these are the kind of cases where he would be investigating. Simply axe-grinding away on Eben Alexander's near-death experience report is not enough.

I move on to some recent observations from the meditation front. One of the pioneering Buddhist (or westernized Buddhist) centers in America is in my hometown of Rochester, New York. The Rochester Zen Center (RZC) was founded by Philip Kapleau (author of the aforementioned *The Three Pillars of Zen*) in 1966 and bills itself as "one of the oldest and largest Zen Buddhist organizations in the United States". I recently attended a workshop and a number of sittings at RZC and report a little from that experience.

First, RZC has on occasion acknowledged its reputation as a "boot camp". So what has earned it that reputation? Well they for the most part still wear Japanese uniforms (although I was allowed to wear simple dark clothing); they apparently follow a number of the norms from Zen centers in Japan from the days of Kapleau's training there in the 1950's (this includes the use of the encouragement stick); and they emphasize plenty of sitting. It is the latter that might be the most noteworthy distinction from other contemporary centers. If you are a fitness center and you really don't offer and house much exercise, then you arguably aren't much of a fitness center. By this analogy I think that plenty of what goes on in contemporary meditation centers only loosely justifies the title "meditation center". A longtime Rochester meditator I ran into had recently gone to a retreat at the local, officially secular version of RZC, the Springwater Center, and reported that 'it would have been nice to have some company in the sitting [or meditation] room'.

I got to hear the teacher at the Rochester Zen Center, Bodhin Kjolhede, give an Easter Sunday talk entitled "Where Christ and Bodhidharma Meet" which was sort of a comparison talk between the secular western Buddhist perspective and that of Christianity (Bodhidharma was as an Indian Buddhist monk who is credited with introducing Chan/Zen Buddhism to China). In particular Bodhin talked about "apophatic theology" using some writings from Thomas Merton. From that perspective God is essentially unknowable and with this Bodhin could make some friendly connections to the ultimate state since Zen is known for its minimalistic descriptions of the awakened state. Bodhin's talk revealed a bit of the contemporary relevant terrain which was nice. At no point in the talk did he acknowledge that Buddhism is a religion, beginning with its life-after-life framework. He did mention that interest in Zen in the West "may have crested" and thus be in decline. Consistent with this he mentioned that it was difficult to get young people to go meditation retreats (which traditionally in Zen are called sesshins). In fact the fervor surrounding RZC since I first came to Rochester in 1983 I would guess - admittedly as an outsider - is down by a factor three or so. In the eighties there were even "Zen houses" in Rochester where lay people focused on Zen practice could live together.

During Bodhin's talk he made some sympathetic comments about atheists, in part suggesting they were being picked on by the religious. Reading between the lines, I think there could be a significant presence of atheists at the Rochester Zen Center and he was simply being friendly to them. From my experiences with online forums addressing the traditional religion of Buddhism versus its common secularized forms, though, the aggressive rude commenting in such forums is more likely to come from the atheist/secular side.

Another relevant point raised by Bodhin in his talk was a purported statement made by Albert Einstein. That statement:

> [t]he religion of the future will be a cosmic religion. It should transcend a personal God and avoid dogmas and a theology. Covering both the natural and the spiritual, it should be based on a religious sense arising from the experience of all things, natural and spiritual as a meaningful whole. If there is any religion that would cope with modern scientific needs, it would be Buddhism [Lopez 6 episodes].

Bodhin was appropriately a bit awkward in delivering this quote as he had to know that the Einstein connection had taken serious flack since there is no documentation to suggest that Einstein really made it. Nonetheless, he went on to add a supportive, "but it sounds like Einstein". I am not qualified to comment on whether it sounds like Einstein, but would simply point out that this infatuation with science/scientists has been around among Western Buddhists for as long as I have been involved. In fact a prominent member of the RZC - and seemingly their designated intellectual - is an atheist physicist (Adam Frank). The relevant Einstein question, though, would seem to be - who would want Einstein's endorsement for something he likely knew next to nothing about and certainly didn't practice? And yet this quote has been used prominently for years by Western Buddhists and still appears to have mileage in it.

Another relevant part of my visit to the Rochester Zen Center was a chance to go to 3 sessions of their "Living and Dying" group. This I was hoping would provide a window into any religious aspects of their practice or purview. The first session passed without touching on the topic of death, it was more akin to a healthy group therapy session (people of course do encounter serious difficulties in their lives and sometimes others in a careful format can provide some helpful tips). The second session was dominated by an individual's concerns over their planned gender-changing agenda and how RZC might better relate to their challenges. At the end of this hour-or-so long session someone raised the issue of death. The questioner was obviously distraught over the death of someone who previously had a prominent connection to RZC. This person's stated concern met with absolute (no pun intended) dead silence. No response at all. At the subsequent breakup of the meeting I talked with that person and mentioned some of purported religious aspects of their chants and practices (which if you bother to notice are framed in a life-after-life perspective). They seemed pleased to hear this and in fact yelled out their window to me as I walked home that day.

The point here is that contrary to the gist of the book, *Waking Up*, even at the relatively conservative Rochester Zen Center, even talking about the religious aspects of Buddhism appears to be off limits. None of my efforts involving sending simple e-mail suggestions on this topic even drew a simple polite acknowledgement or response. This is also largely consistent with my other sendings to people involved with Western Buddhism including academics. One notable exception involved an ex-member of RZC who seemed genuinely interested and even sent me a couple of thoughtful followup notes. For additional context here, RZC is where the late teacher Toni Packer was trained and eventually made the controversial declaration that she wanted nothing to do with the religion Buddhism (she was in part influenced by the non-religious teachings of the previously mentioned Jiddu Krishnamurti). So she and some other RZC members left the center to establish an officially secular meditation center which is now the previously mentioned Springwater Center. Toni's exit from RZC - and its purportedly deleterious Buddhist rituals - happened in 1981. I am still not sure it really mattered as the Springwater Center certainly has not thrived and their nominal goal is still the same as RZC's - to try to facilitate waking up. Moreover from what I gathered in my visits to the Rochester Zen Center those rituals are essentially motivated in secular terms in that they are essentially claimed to further the focus necessary for an enlightenment experience.

So in 1981 a significant meditation teacher leaves a prominent Western (minimally) Buddhist center to go establish a secular-only center and in 2014 Sam Harris purports to try to start the secularization "conversation" in the West. Additionally, that teacher was from a German intellectual background and tried to keep up with relevant scientific literature. Also, Toni was friendly person and must have allowed me to have 10 to 20 hours of conversations with her. One of her acknowledged frustration points was that it is very difficult to get people to have enlightenment experiences (any such experience, forget lasting significant ones). And I would suggest that Toni's/Springwater's approach ended up being rather casual not unlike the minimally determined approach espoused in *Waking Up* (which may be quite common now). The relevant logic to this contemporary approach appears to be - why pursue a state that you can assume you already have? In the case of the Springwater Center from what I saw a few years ago on a visit there that can entail going to a retreat and maybe sitting a few hours a day in meditation. And of course forget being encouraged to make determined efforts. As appears to be pretty common these days, the meditation at Springwater is unfocused and seemingly cliche-oriented, and I suggest likely to be minimally effective. At one point during a retreat discussion period at the Springwater Center the three residing meditation teachers simultaneously turned to me and exhorted "Shhhh!". What offense had I committed? I suggested that the meditation process entailed "work".

B. Some Conclusions About Meditation

I wind up here with some personal observations and then a few conclusions following some quotes on meditation. Getting started with observations, probably the most significant reason to try some meditation is to explore paying attention in a fuller sense. Indirectly we all pay attention but this appears to involve externally-directed, focused efforts. To safely drive a vehicle it requires a certain amount of focused attention. Likewise many work activities require focused attention. On this point I wonder if one of the big contributors to the satisfaction that can come from working simply comes from the requisite focused state.

If you are interested you can of course find some meditation classes or programs to attend. I recommend trying to find something that is low-key and un-hyped. One of my most memorable experiences as a student was in some sessions with a man simply teaching attention. Although highly trained via Tibetan monastics, his teachings involved simple awareness (or paying attention) exercises. Nothing extra, just the exercises at hand along with his sincere commentary. Enlightenment was not mentioned. Trying to pay attention turns out to be very challenging; in its own mundane way enlightening; and can also be rewarding. Additionally some of the classes I have attended with older Tibetan teachers - which naturally included some religious context - were likewise sincere and involved minimal hype or ego.

Simple introductory practices typically involve paying attention to some internal process. This might entail silently counting your breath or just paying attention to (or following) your breath. My first meditation practice involved silently repeating a short word phrase or mantra. The idea is to try to patiently and persistently stay with your meditational focus. It is sounds easy but is not. Our minds are inclined towards wondering and our attention is very easily caught up in the wondering. To facilitate the process it is typically recommended that you sit up relatively straight and have a quiet bland setting. I usually sit on a meditation cushion and stare downward towards an adjacent blank wall. Although I have done this for years, the basic recurrence of catching your mind wandering and then starting again with the focus continues to this day. Another form of formal meditation involves walking while staying focused on a practice. Along these lines, I regularly pace back and forth in my living room in quiet fashion.

An initial breakthrough aspect of the process is that you can come to vividly realize that our default mind state is self-sustained distraction (i.e., 'blah-blah-blah-me, blah-blah-blah-me, …'). As a result I am regularly amazed when intellectuals like Steven Pinker express grand views of the mind and thinking. For a relevant illustration consider a trip to a grocery store. When I visit they are invariably playing some kind of background music and invariably it draws some kind of mental reaction. Unless I am trying to pay attention I tend to get caught up in responding. If I like the song then I may start humming or quietly singing along. That initial process I think provides an introduction to how our internal distraction happens. We perceive and then react to external (or internal) stimuli and this in turn elicits an orchestra of internal followup including memories and of course emotions. Unfortunately, this default cyclical wandering or grasping mindstate can really dilute our experience of life and also the habitual blah-blah-blah mind routine can unconsciously lock us into our repetitive behavioral grooves and insensitivities (including perhaps limiting our appreciation of music). Furthermore, I have found that my stream of consciousness is rarely creative.

On a particular point here, Sam Harris repeatedly identifies the crux of the matter as entailing our identifying with thought. But getting caught up with external phenomena - like the music at the grocery store - does not really involve identifying with it. The underlying detour which our minds' are so susceptible to, entails grasping at perceivable phenomena (internal or external) and almost immediately reacting with some memory-based response. This whole process can cycle along at a minimally conscious level. By minimizing external distractions, formal meditation allows the underlying mind mechanics to become more apparent and in that we can become a bit wiser to our incessant internal Talk Radio tendencies. This is ultimately a humbling process but it can facilitate some helpful quiet clarity or awareness.

A basic point here is that I suggest meditators - even experienced ones - not abandon a simple daily focused practice. Maybe for lay practice that is the best way to go. The contemporary trends seem to emphasize unfocused or open meditation but I think that comes at a real cost. A simple focus - such as trying to follow your breath or counting your breath (up to 10 and then starting over) - offers a practical exercise in simple internal awareness and also a healthy dose of realism. You might think of this as a simple daily mind calisthenic. The alternative open style, perhaps akin to multitasking, can easily be a dilute or distracted experience. I saw recently that the American meditation teacher Adyashanti commented that many of the experienced meditators he was encountering had difficulty simply focusing or concentrating. Without a daily focused practice this can easily happen as I have observed with my own efforts. Perhaps the ultimate related challenge with any sincere meditation practice - or other spiritual practices - is to try to balance the need for focusing with the complementary need for openness. They are both important aspects of healthy living and their balancing seems like an ongoing vital art.

Moving along here to comment on a potential longer term challenge with meditation practice. If you are seriously committed to ongoing meditation efforts then you may want to see the book, *After the Ecstasy, the Laundry*, by the American meditation teacher Jack Kornfeld. That book sheds some light on the fact that with sustained meditation efforts there can be significant sub-enlightenment breakthroughs - sometimes termed openings - but that in the subsequent lay realm they can be upended in a big way. There really are under-discussed challenges with regards to serious lay meditation practice (which might be consistent with the traditional low-key emphasis on lay meditation).

If you are interested in trying a meditational practice you might consider looking for some experienced and humble help. Amongst the predominant secular contemporary scene this might not be easy. But among the traditional religious approaches the challenge might be more in connecting the practice or teachings to your everyday life. Living a sane everyday life is not easy and it is probably a good idea to be pleased with whatever help you can get. In addition to my meditation/paying-attention practice I also try to get outside regularly. I find that outdoor walks can really be therapeutic and somewhat of a meditative experience.

I add some final meditation commentary. There are a number of good books attempting to help people with an interest in meditating. On the other hand there are plenty of superficial ones. One tendency is to sell meditation/enlightenment in a superficial and even effortless way. That approach is not realistic. Another unhelpful approach is the tendency to pander to science or scientism. *Waking Up* is not alone in demonstrating this tendency. A recent popular book by Robert Wright entitled *Why Buddhism is True: The Science and Philosophy of Meditation and Enlightenment* papers appears to be based on the author's need to make sure that Buddhist meditation is scientifically kosher. This tendency was also captured in a line in an article by a Western teacher who claimed that that he and many other modern Buddhists experience "profound embarrassment" over Buddhism's rebirth belief, but satisfaction over Buddhism's apparent "resonance with quantum physics, cutting edge neuroscience, and modern rationality" [Spellmeyer]. I have to admit to being embarrassed that something that I am involved with is home to so much intellectual-wannabe-ism.

One book that is particularly helpful is Shunryu Suzuki's *Zen Mind, Beginner's Mind*. A simple but also subtle book derived from talks given during Zen meditation retreats (and "enlightenment" only shows up in passing). Suzuki opened his Prologue with:

> People say that practicing Zen is difficult, but there is a misunderstanding as to why. It is not difficult because it is hard to sit in the cross-legged position, or to attain enlightenment. It is difficult because it is hard to keep your mind pure and our practice pure in its fundamental sense [Suzuki, p.1].

First, his opening two "not difficult" assertions are in fact difficult, but perhaps this was done to emphasize the third point. The "cross-legged position" that he refers to is later identified in the first talk as being the full lotus posture! I have repeatedly asserted about the difficulty of encountering enlightenment experiences. But the emphasized latter point is a very good one and Suzuki closed his Prologue with this elaboration on what pure implies:

> So, the most difficult thing is always to keep your beginner's mind. There is no need to have a deep understanding of Zen. Even though you read much Zen literature, you must read each sentence with a fresh mind. You should not say, "I know what Zen is," or "I have attained enlightenment." This is also the secret of the arts: always be a beginner. Be very very careful about this point. If you start to practice zazen, you will begin to appreciate your beginner's mind. It is the secret of Zen practice [Suzuki, pp.2-3].

People at the talks he gave (and likely the presumed readers of his book) were already doing some meditation (although they may not be sitting in full lotus!). His point here (and repeated throughout the book) is that the big picture goal is trying to stay with life closely and attentively, analogous to what a beginner might do. That is the goal and it isn't an easy one. His Zen center, by the way, emphasized meditation focused on following the breath. Finally, although his commentary might have been a bit language-limited, it covered many aspects of engaged living and is simply outstanding.

Another helpful book is the aforementioned *I AM THAT* involving conversations with Sri Nisargadatta Maharaj. Nisargadatta seems to have plumbed the depth of meditation and with it gotten a bird's eyes view of our inner psyches and difficulties. If you stay with meditation practice in a sustained way then you have a good chance of getting a front row seat on your inner dramas and dynamics, which otherwise tend to make themselves known indirectly thru our outer compulsions. Nisargadatta, although without a formal education, somehow seemed to be exceptionally lucid in providing suggestions with regards to this inner landscape, as well as the deeper freedom possible thru an awakening experience. Below is an extended excerpt from a discussion that took place at his meditation abode (which was located upstairs from his modest small store). Of note here is that the references to "pain" might be motivated in part by the discomfort or soreness sitters often face in extended meditation efforts. Sitting may look boring but that is rarely the case. Continuing, "Q" designates the questioner and "M" designates Nisargadatta (the Maharaj). Here goes:

> Q: Do you advise shunning pleasure and pursuing pain?
>
> M: No, nor pursuing pleasure and shunning pain. Accept both as they come, enjoy both while they last, let them go, as they must.
>
> Q: How can I possibly enjoy pain? Physical pain calls for action.
>
> M: Of course. And so does mental. The bliss is in the awareness of it, in not shrinking, or in any way turning away from it. All happiness comes from awareness. The more we are conscious, the deeper the joy. Acceptance of pain, non-resistance, courage and endurance - these open deep and perennial sources of real happiness, true bliss.
>
> Q: Why should pain be more effective than pleasure?

> M: Pleasure is readily accepted, while all the powers of the self reject pain. As acceptance of pain is the denial of the self, and self stands in the way of true happiness, the wholehearted acceptance of pain releases the springs of happiness.
>
> Q: Does the acceptance of suffering act the same way?
>
> M: The fact of pain is easily brought within the focus of awareness. With suffering it is not that simple. To focus [on] suffering is not enough, for mental life, as we know it, is one continuous stream of suffering. To reach the deeper layers of suffering you must go to its roots and uncover their vast underground network, where fear and desire are closely interwoven and the currents of life's energy oppose, obstruct and destroy each other.
>
> Q: How can I set right a tangle which is entirely below the level of my consciousness?
>
> M: My being with yourself, the 'I am'; by watching yourself in your daily life with alert interest, with the intention to understand rather than judge, in full acceptance of whatever may emerge, because it is there, you encourage the deep to come to the surface and enrich your life and consciousness with its captive energies. This is the great work of awareness; it removes obstacles and releases energies by understanding the nature of life and mind. Intelligence is the door to freedom and alert attention is the mother of intelligence [Nisargadatta, p.278].

This passage captures a good chunk of the general spirit of meditative inquiry. You sit and try to stay present (and a focal practice can help with that), and then stay there come what may. Note that along with the suggestion, "encourag[ing] of the deep to come to the surface", is an implied (but stated elsewhere) point that one doesn't act out impulsively in harmful or distracting ways. In a simple everyday sense I think as adults we all know this routine. Sometimes deeply committed efforts involving stuff we can not turn back from, as for example being a parent or a friend in a difficult situation, can paradoxically be excruciating, liberating, and rewarding. The relevant advice in such circumstances is commonly to "Hang in there".

Continuing with this everyday parallel, I remember in Andrew Solomon's *Far From the Tree* one episode dealt with a women who had been seriously tested by her Down syndrome child. In asking about her observations from her work with other parents in similar circumstances, and in particular did they share her energetic engagement, she commented, "[t]hey all do. That's the wild thing about special needs parents. This comes raging out of you. I feel such strength and courage in these women" [Solomon, p.198]. Likewise when people stay committed to meditation (or other forms of engaged living) it can facilitate hanging in there and meeting life's inevitable challenges (including of course pain). One of the miracles that such work can help uncover, is that painful situations can somehow transform themselves and you can come to appreciate a little of Nisargadatta's final characterization above. On this point it is worth noting that the Japanese man, Ittetsu Nemoto, in the aforementioned *New Yorker* article had his seemingly miraculous energetic awakening experience following a profound hanging-in-there episode. Something apparently untangled itself within him and a remarkable energetic burst arose.

The traditional framing of such meditation practices is largely within a life-after-life perspective. One practices so that one can further appreciate life's lessons, facilitate helping others, and grow some - in what might be described as a spiritual sense. I think traditionally people involved in such practices didn't expect some final enlightenment breakthrough in the current lifetime and certainly not in an easy fashion. The traditional modesty in such matters could simply reflect realism. On that note I suggest that very few contemporary teachers - certainly in the West - have more than a superficial feel for Suzuki's or certainly Nisargadatta's teachings.

CHAPTER 5 - CONCLUSIONS

I wind down here and make a few more points in the wake of the previous essays. It is not difficult to question science's material-only vision of life. Contradicting the certitude of science there are bunch of behavioral phenomena which are very difficult to explain from a materialist perspective. The inability of science to acknowledge this situation contradicts the regularly proclaimed openness and curiosity of scientists. In fact science has its own rigid materialist purview and strongly defends it.

Beyond the mostly peripheral behavioral anomalies, though, there are large questions with regards to the plausibility of the functioning of DNA. This book has pointed out the gross failures encountered in attempting to connect DNA to many of our heritable characteristics, in particular with regards to our innate behavioral tendencies. In an analogous vein, some like the banished scientist Rupert Sheldrake, have focused on the need for additional physical factors to explain the form and functioning of organisms. On this point Sheldrake has an outstanding bet against a claim made by biologist Lewis Wolpert [Sheldrake bet]. Wolpert's claim is that:

> [b]y 1 May 2029, given the genome of a fertilized egg of an animal or plant, we will be able to predict in at least one case all the details of the organism that develops from it, including any abnormalities.

After acknowledging the enormous complexity of organisms, Wolpert went on to add that:

> [t]o win the bet, we will have to be able to predict the behavior of almost all the cells in the embryo. In a small worm, say the nematode Caenorhabditis elegans, there are 959 cells, making it the ideal model to solve this problem. It is a major challenge, but advances in cell biology, systems biology and computing will take us there.

Sheldrake, though, is not buying this and began his response by simply stating "Wolpert's faith in the predictive power of the genome is misplaced". He went on to elaborate on the enormous complexity hurdles facing DNA. In the end Sheldrake pointed out that:

> Wolpert is not alone in believing in the predictive value of the genome. Governments, venture capitalists and medical charities have bet and are still betting billions of dollars on it. More than a case of fine port [the wine wager] is at stake.

I greatly appreciate Rupert Sheldrake's efforts - not the least because he sincerely tries to be polite despite his banishment from science - but I disagree with the particulars here. Instead I offer my own conclusion:

> there are profound innate differences in human behavioral tendencies and those differences are supposed to largely be derived from differences in DNA. Given the very limited amount of variable DNA that we possess; the comprehensive failure of extensive searches thru that variable DNA; and the officially stated genomic expectations: it is now reasonable to conclude that genomic behavioral success is not going to happen. A parallel situation has unfolded with the expectations of personal genomics. This represents a basic failure of the scientific understanding of life and by implication its evolution.

Given the nature of the behavioral challenge - including a big spread in innate intellectual abilities down to very specific behavioral shifts as found with autism or the transgender phenomena - something significant DNA-wise should already have been identified. I am thus confident of the failure of the existing DNA model. Some other factors have to be involved.

For additional perspective here I am suggesting that a bet about a genomic-based prediction for a 959 cell worm extending forward 10 years, is simply to too little and too late. The relevant human challenge is embodied in personal genomics and behavioral genetics. That is where the gross shortcomings of the genetics-heredity model are now apparent. Of additional note is that there is little need to read the genetics literature. In such literature the relevant sober findings are harder to uncover. In popular literature like *Scientific American* or the *New York Times* relevant synopses are more transparent, which to this day might best be together titled "The Missing Heritability Continues To Go Missing".

For people interested in investigating religious or alternative understanding of life this is where I think you should be focusing. If science's materialist or molecular-only vision is accurate then how much mystery is available with regards to life? Perhaps some rare unusual behaviors here and there (and of course subjectivity!). If DNA strike out, though, it suggests science is wrong about life in a broad way. From a religious perspective there could be some unidentified top-down (God or gods) contributions and/or from the complementary bottom-up (souls) perspective there could be additional contributions. In a simple way I think monozygotic twins embody the unfolding mystery. In a superficial physical appearance way they are almost identical as expected from a materialist perspective (Check). In a deeper way though, beginning with personality they are not (No Check). It would be nice to think that some serious academic intellectuals would be chomping at the bit to investigate this situation.

Moving on to another perspective here I suggest this situation is also inherently practical in nature. Beyond the Who-We-Are and What-Happens-To-Us mysteries implied by the missing heritability problem, there are also possible significant societal implications. Here I am reminded of a fine review of an E. O. Wilson book that I read in *Scientific American* several years ago. As is not uncommon in such future-oriented, science-based books E. O. Wilson's conjured up some optimism in his conclusions with regards to humanity's unfolding sustainability and eco-management crises. The reviewer was also a biologist and they rejected Wilson's optimism. That reviewer concluded humans beings will not make significant sacrifices for future people. Given the material-only, this-life-only, and associated selfish take on human beings, the biologist reviewer's negative conclusion makes sense. Deeper investigations of human beings (and animals), though, might find rationale for different perspectives. With the common premodern transcendental perspective, in which souls tend to cycle thru lives, our existential logic could be different.

Somewhat consistent with this in Michael Tobias' searing man-versus-nature epic, *World War III*, the group identified for their encouraging sustainability and ecological priorities were the lay Jains. Their religion, Jainism, presents a world view of underlying souls cycling thru lives and a belief in the sanctity of all those souls. Souls are even posited for plants. In any case a very high priority for Jains is to minimize the suffering imposed on other souls (which can lead to apparent excess among the monastics and also some complicated ethical logic). The ultimate personal religious goal is to achieve freedom from reincarnation and the associated ignorance. This is believed to be a huge task as can be gleaned from a synopsis [Jainworld]. Paired with that personal goal is a goal of assisting other beings in doing the same. In any case, Tobias' discussion suggests that Jains tend to have a very good disposition towards the ecology and sustainability challenges. Unlike *Enlightenment Now*, Tobais' book was based on his extensive travel and personal investigations.

I add some of my own observations. In the past I used to eat lunch with a highly educated, non-religious person. That person was clear about the threat associated with climate change but they had little concern about it. Of the situation they said simply, 'I'll be gone before it gets serious'. That person for further context here was a long time committed participant in secular Buddhism and also had a part-time connection to the nuclear power industry. From the backdrop of this book's essays, this person had very solid credentials to be considered Enlightened in the traditional Western sense, and perhaps even a bit enlightened in the (westernized-)Eastern sense. And yet they had minimal concern about climate change and thus their perspective seems consistent with the conclusions of the aforementioned biologist reviewer. Furthermore as a relatively educated person who has spent a good deal of time around other relatively educated and nominally Enlightened people, I must say I am not optimistic that the Enlightened/intellectual perspective is adequate to meeting the motivational demands of our unfolding eco-crisis.

A basic point raised by Steven Pinker in *Enlightenment Now* is of the supposedly progressive inclinations of modern secular people. In fact if that were true - beyond the kind of trendy intellectualisms we all partake in - then we would not be facing the crises we are. My sense is that it is not that hard to live a simpler, truly progressive life if motivated sufficiently. As a society we are not doing this.

Now shifting back to the contemporary intellectual perception of science. During the fall of 2019 I can still read for the most part highly positive Amazon reader reviews of Siddhartha Mukherjee's *The Gene*. Mukherjee's its-in-the-DNA conclusions were certainly questionable in 2016 and one might think that with his stated "end of the decade" prediction that readers in the fall of 2019 might question it. Wrong, though, science seems to have won out with its hubris-framed vision. Here is a relatively sober review from September 16, 2019 titled "Amazing book!":

> [t]his is an amazing, well-researched and well-written book. As a scientist and researcher myself, I loved the detail wrapped in storytelling. I learned a lot and complex information is presented is presented in a way that's understandable.

A number of the other reviews are simply over-the top nonsense. Some of the titles included "The most fascinating book that I've ever read", "A must read", "Providential read!", and "Became my favorite book". If readers want a quick tour of the prominent footprint or wake of contemporary scientism then you might read some of those reviews. Questioning the scientific vision of life is for the most part not happening, and instead reveling and/or simply applauding it appears to be a strong tendency (at least for the educated).

Earlier in the book I suggested there were two big areas of pure science. The first area is centered on biology and here materialism is a fixture. The other is physics and materialism is even more of a fixture. Mark Gober in his *The End of Upside Down Thinking* gives some samples of the utter contempt for paranormal reports found amongst physicists [Gober, p.195, pp.197-98]. When your research area is highly speculative and incredibly remote from life you are not likely to want hear about everyday jaw-dropping psychic phenomena. Furthering the situation is that physics has created for itself a largely unquestioned role as the final intellectual arbitrator of what reality is and with this a role in defining the true frontiers of knowledge (although somewhat of an emerging peer is now neuroscience).

I now critically approach contemporary physics in a tangential fashion. As a kid for a while I really enjoyed reading about amazing feats such as those chronicled in *Ripley's Believe it or Not!* and the *Guinness Book of World Records*. After a few years, though, I came to see the process as rather empty. I would get a short term cerebral Wow!-kick thinking about some unlikely happenings, but it didn't change anything for me or likely even the participants. Years later as an adult I saw an article about a graduating senior who was gushing about her subsequent plans to study the 'philosophical implications of quantum mechanics'. Something then clicked as it dawned on me that much of the attention on modern physics could really be an analogous 'Wow! Think of that!'-phenomena. Also overlapping with this might be the near worship-like following associated with the presumed brilliance of physicists. Albert Einstein and his work probably were big contributors to this phenomena.

One of the big epicenters of physics hype has to be quantum speculation. Even as an outsider it was readily apparent that physicists in general did not want to change the status quo with regards to the crazy speculation derived from the loose and contradictory Copenhagen Interpretation. Thus, for example a relatively mundane description (or ontology) as suggested by David Bohm (and earlier Louis De Broglie) was rudely stiff-armed out of general recognition by mainstream physicists [Peat; Carroll NYT]. In somewhat of an analogous effort, a friend and colleague from academic work, Alan Kadin, has carefully shown that a number of what he refers to as "rupture[s] in the unified fabric of physics" can be coherently approached by beginning with a coherent wave-based description of an electron and its spin [Kadin]. Kadin found it nearly impossible to get relevant manuscripts published. Similarly, Sean Carroll pointed out that, "for years, the leading journal in physics had an explicit policy that papers on the foundations of quantum mechanics were to be rejected out of hand" [Carroll NYT].

I think this research impasse could well have had a significant ego basis for it. If quantum mechanics were explained in relatively normal terms - for example something akin to Maxwell's Equations - then what would that do to the current hype surrounding physics? Would there be undergraduate's - and perhaps significantly female ones - gushing about its philosophical implications? Would there be ongoing super-hyped speculation surrounding it?

From that I move on to make a comment about contemporary physics based on some recent work by Sean Carroll. In my earlier book I wrote a little about his book, *The Big Picture*. In it Carroll naturally dismisses any possible paranormal or non-materialist aspect of life as impossible given the understanding of contemporary physics and thus apparently making it not even worth reading about. Further, as is the custom in such science-based works, he had to include some discussions attempting to humanize a vision of life that ultimately can be characterized completely in terms of an equation (and those discussions drew an early sharp critical review from an Amazon customer based on the nature of those "Pollyanna-isms") [Pollyanna]. Elsewhere in fact, Carroll has characterized everything as coming down to "in truth, only atoms and the void" [Carroll blog]. Carroll's most recent book, *Something Deeply Hidden: Quantum Worlds and the Emergence of Spacetime*, plunges into physics' designated hype realm, the aforementioned foundations of quantum mechanics. Here is the text from the inside front jacket:

> As you read these words, copies of you are being created.
>
> Sean Carroll, theoretical physicist and one of this world's most celebrated writers on science, rewrites the history of 20th century physics. Already hailed as a masterpiece, *Something Deeply Hidden* shows for the first time that facing up to the essential puzzle of quantum mechanics utterly transforms how we think about space and time. His reconciling of quantum mechanics with Einstein's theory of relativity changes, well, everything.
>
> Most physicists haven't even recognized the uncomfortable truth: physics has been in crisis since 1927. Quantum mechanics has always had obvious gaps - which have come to be simply ignored. Science popularizers keep telling us how weird it is, how impossible it is to understand. Academics discourage students from working on the "dead end" of quantum foundations. Putting his professional reputation on the line with his audacious yet entirely reasonable book, Carroll says that the crisis can now come to an end. We just have to accept that there is more than one of us in the universe. There are many, many Sean Carrolls. Many of every one of us.
>
> Copies of you are generated thousands of times per second. The Many Worlds Theory of quantum behavior says that every time there is a quantum event, a world splits off with everything in it the same, except in that other world the quantum event didn't happen. Step-by-step in Carroll's uniquely lucid way, he tackles the major objections to this otherworldly revelation until his case is inescapably established.
>
> Rarely does a book so fully reorganize how we think about our place in the universe[s]. We are on the threshold of a new understanding - of where we are in the cosmos[s], and what we are made of.

This is truly spectacular hype about what can only be described as extraordinary speculations. Even within the Many Worlds description there is a glaring error. It isn't "worlds" being split off, it is (entire) universes. For a sampling of its possible everyday implications interested readers might try spending a day or two actively contemplating these purported universe splittings. You might consider giving the speculation a pause, though, when operating a vehicle in traffic. Readers might also reflect back on the earlier quote by Ricky Gervais on the purported sober and "humble" nature of science.

Earlier this book considered some taboo or paranormal phenomena. Here I add a little followup. There are many such fascinating topics that have been roped off from nominally respectable consideration. One such area has involved cases of young children who appear to recall previous lives. I really liked Jim Tucker's *Life Before Life* but the big source of many of the investigated cases was his former colleague, Ian Stevenson. In an appraisal of Ian Stevenson's research on this matter the *Scientific American* blogger, Jesse Bering, wrote in an entry entitled "Ian Stevenson's Case for the Afterlife: Are We Skeptics Really Just Cynics?" that:

> when you actually read [the cases] firsthand, many are exceedingly difficult to explain away by rational, non-paranormal means. Much of this is due to Ian Stevenson's own exhaustive efforts to disconfirm the paranormal account. "We can strive towards objectivity by exposing as fully as possible all observations that tend to weaken our preferred interpretation of the data," he wrote. "If adversaries fire at us, let them use ammunition that we have given them." And if truth be told, he excelled at debunking the debunkers.

Bering also cited the support of one prominent scientist, physicist Doris Kuhlmann-Wilsdorf, who found that Stevenson's work provided "overwhelming" evidence for the existence of reincarnation. A more recent and extraordinarily detailed case is chronicled in *Soul Survivor: The Reincarnation of a World War II Fighter Pilot* by Bruce and Andrea Leininger (with Ken Gross) (Leininger and Leininger 2009). In Leininger's book they chronicled their experiences with their son as he appeared to vividly recall traumatic experiences as a World War II fighter pilot. The strength of their case was significantly boosted by the fact that the devout Catholic father, Bruce, went to amazing lengths to investigate the possible reincarnation explanation in hopes of debunking it. I add that ironically it would seem unlikely that official investigators will stumble on a case as supportive as the Leininger's case.

Additional support for the reincarnation hypothesis could be provided by therapy observations like those described by the psychiatrist Brian Weiss in his book *Many Lives, Many Masters* [Weiss]. Neither Weiss nor the patient that he wrote about believed in reincarnation, but their hypnosis-based push back in time appeared to uncover reincarnation consistent-memories. Weiss had simply suggested going back further in time and his patient then appeared to vividly recall some striking events (many of them deaths). *Many Lives, Many Masters* appears to contain a number of sincere and remarkable reports. Weiss' also reported that these apparent intense recalls seemed to help his patient resolve their phobias.

Jesse Bering's above comment that "many are exceedingly difficult to explain away by rational, non-paranormal means" if truth be told might be applied across a number of paranormal categories. It is a measure of their materialist fixation that the majority in the science camp can not even consider such reports, whilst a theory suggesting universes replicating themselves zillions of times per second apparently is. Personally, I have found Ian Stevenson's reincarnation work (as well as some others in the ostracized paranormal research camp) annoyingly overdone. Does anyone in the real world or even the formality-bent academic psychology world have to vet phenomena so thoroughly? On this point it is worth noting my entire memory- or anecdote-based recall of my life's events seems to remarkably align itself with those of other family members (although we differ in the emotional significances of some events).

On the other hand, exceptional but accepted behaviors appear to provide an alternative simpler means for challenging materialism, in part due to the ongoing or continuous nature of such behaviors. Musical prodigies do not display their prowess in unpredictable blips, it is an ongoing readily observable phenomena and mystery. The same is true with the gender orientation of transgender children.

Overall, Elizabeth Mayer's *Extraordinary Knowing* really impressed me both for its range of topics and also its sincerity. The reports involving psychics or intuitive-s were amazing and perhaps simply echo earlier analogous reports. Chris Carter's *Science and the Afterlife Experience* was also impressive in particular with its rather thorough look at efforts to communicate with the deceased. This topic is currently so taboo few will apparently write about it, but Carter on the other hand took a serious look at it. Some of the supporting evidence, including getting very high level chess-playing out of a non-chess-playing medium who was purportedly communicating with a deceased grandmaster, was impressive. Other examples included efforts to communicate to some notable deceased figures and the associated efforts to validate the purported communication. Some of the validation analyses included efforts seemingly initiated by the disembodied figures. It is unfortunate that more people are not open to reading about such notable efforts. Such activity might be rare but they certainly challenges contemporary assumptions about life as well as offering some unreligious observations about possible post-death experiences.

Another large paranormal topic relates to near-death experiences. My sense is that a lot of that work gets extrapolated too positively, in part reflecting the gravitational pull of specific religious beliefs (as reflected in Eben Alexander's book title, *Proof of Heaven*). You can certainly get that sense if you follow the work of an organization like the International Organization for Near Death Studies (IANDS). For myself I think that our innate religious perspectives as chronicled in *Born Believers* offers a more general spiritual possibility. Instead of looking to relatively rare, perhaps selectively upbeat, short term visions that purport to look beyond the edge of biological life; you might instead notice that we appear to somehow come into life with an innate spiritual perspective. Such a perspective might then be consistent with our having been around the life-death block (so to speak) and maintained some memories of the intervening disembodied experience. One possible thread across embodiments could be personality which has been observed to vary in many species [Angier]. Nonetheless, whatever the quality of a possible disembodied experience, if we are likely to be pulled back into embodiment then perhaps this is where our attention and priorities belong.

I conclude here with some observations of refugee adults that I have interacted via my tutoring efforts. First, almost all of these adults come from very different backgrounds than most Americans, certainly relatively educated Americans. The refugees appear to be tougher than we are. In a relevant example one refugee told me that at her place of work (entailing demanding manual labor in a manufacturing effort) - 'all of the employees are Asian refugees' (although management is American). In somewhat of a parallel, I have rarely in my life met such quietly determined people as some of the East African refugee tutoring assistants that I have worked with. Furthermore, a number of the refugees I have observed seem to be content to live relatively hard-working modest lives. On this point I am left with a sense that we Americans have largely drifted towards being relatively spoiled and as least physically, lazy.

Another distinction I have noticed is with physical posture. Some of the refugee ladies (admittedly men don't show up much to pick up kids at the library) appear anchored to good posture. You can see this when they sit on a flat chair and naturally support themselves in an erect healthy fashion. One of the refugee moms I have observed sitting cross-legged on the floor and maintaining what to me is close to perfect posture in an ongoing fashion. By this I mean managing to sit with her butt on the floor whilst having her legs crossed in front of her and simultaneously maintaining what appears like outstanding posture even for a standing person. This includes of course what seems like an ideal lumbar curvature (readers might try doing this for themselves). And her attitude is completely non-pretentious as though maintaining excellent posture were something akin to breathing - a simple vital practice.

It would certainly be an excellent lifetime habit to instill in order to potentially push back against the back difficulties commonly experienced in the modern world (and thus the regular warnings about the dangers of sitting). One thing I have noticed about the aging process in America is that posture is sort of a visible measure. That is that the older people get the lousier their posture is. This includes being bent forward at the waist and also with regards to the neck being bent forward. How many Americans recognize the importance of maintaining good posture? Perhaps some in the armed services. Furthermore, how many Americans actually pursue good posture? Not just passive with lumbar support but also actively maintaining good posture.

I add some of my own relevant experience. In my upbringing I do not remember anyone saying anything about posture other than perhaps an occasional crude directive from a teacher - 'Sit up.' As a senior in high school I managed to injure my lower back. Eventually I went thru the Enlightened process and got to see some big shot doctor from the Boston area (I think he had a position at Massachusetts General Hospital). He gave me a dismal perspective (it will hurt for the rest of your life) and a presumably good strategy minimize the problem. That strategy was to boycott any lumbar curvature and keep my lower back as straight as possible. As a naive youth at the time I dutifully followed this idiot strategy and maintained a flat lower back (and also maintained the pain). After over a year my father (who occasionally questions Enlightened ways) took me to see a chiropractor. That chiropractor managed to offer me a counterstrategy and some optimism. That counterstrategy was to try to encourage back the original lumbar curve. This worked like a charm (the logic is not subtle as lumbar curvature tends to work against the possibility of disc material getting pushed out into spinal nerves).

The long term situation wasn't so charming, though. Changing your posture ultimately means changing the ligaments that establish the base position of the vertebra. My corrective posturing efforts had managed to pinch in the pain-inflicting bottom disc but still left the overall curve of my lumbar vertebra flat. This ended up causing a lot of difficulty and eventually a big detour into serious corrective efforts (on my own). Anyway these relatively uneducated refugees apparently grew up with a bedrock priority of maintaining good posture. The one lady in particular who left me flabbergasted by sitting crosslegged on the floor with perfect posture, never attended school and happens to be Muslim. Is it even imaginable that educated people in the West would take her posture-based lifestyle and lessons seriously, say compared with a big resume-wielding Western orthopedist?

I close my writing here with my sense that modern educated people have tended to block off a lot of older useful insights and also perspectives on life. Arrogance is rarely justified and should be questioned. I think modern science has been a big player in this dynamic.

ABOUT THE AUTHOR

Ted Christopher lives in Rochester, New York. He has held a variety of jobs including some academic-based, biomedical ultrasound research efforts. Post-high school, his formal education has been mostly technical and included a PhD in Electrical Engineering. Concurrent with these efforts he has tried to make sense of some basic aspects of life, perhaps influenced by his involvement with Buddhist practices and more generally his religious instincts.

Acknowledgments

The author gratefully acknowledges the Central Library of Rochester and Monroe County. A number of significant books were obtained at that library. Some of these books were encountered on one of Central's new books tables. The librarian Andrew Coyle was particularly helpful in obtaining books and also offering some suggestions. The Central Library continues to offer a good reading space.

Some editing feedback was provided by Cindi Rittenhouse. I am very grateful for her efforts but in the end take responsibility for any errors. Additionally, Brian Schwartz and selfpublish.org were very helpful in getting the book published.

REFERENCES

Allegrini A. G., Selzam S., Rimfeld K., von Stumm S., Pingault J. B., and Plomin R. Genomic prediction of cognitive traits in childhood and adolescence. *Molecular Psychiatry*, April 11 2019. Available at https://www.biorxiv.org/content/10.1101/418210v1. Accessed on February 19, 2020.

Almass A. H. *Essence With The Elixir of Enlightenment: The Diamond Approach to Inner Realization.* Newburyport, MA: Weiser Books, 1998.

Angier N. Even Among Animals: Leaders, Followers, and Schmoozers. New York Times, April 5, 2010.

Austin J. *Zen and the Brain: Toward an Understanding of Meditation and Consciousness.* Cambridge, MA: The MIT Press; 1998.

Balter M. *Schizophrenia's Unyielding Mysteries.* Scientific American, May 2017.

Bar-On Y. M., Phillips R., and Milo R. The biomass distribution on Earth. Available online at www.pnas.org/cgi/doi/10.1073/pnas.1711842115. Accessed on November 21, 2019.

Barrett J. L. *Born Believers - The Science of Children's Religious Belief.* New York, NY: Free Press; 2012.

Berg J. J., Harpak A., Sinnott-Armstrong N., Joergensen A. M., Mostafavi H., Field Y., Boyle E. A., Zhang X., Racimo F., Pritchard J. K., and Coop G. Reduced signal for polygenic adaptation of height in UK Biobank. *eLife*, March 21, 2019. Available at https://elifesciences.org/articles/39725 . Accessed on February 19, 2020.

Bering J. Ian Stevenson's Case for the Afterlife: Are We Skeptics Really Just Cynics? Scientific American blog entry November 2013. https://blogs.scientificamerican.com/bering-in-mind/ian-stevensone28099s-case-for-the-afterlife-are-we-e28098skepticse28099-really-just-cynics/. Accessed on December 9, 2019.

Bering J. One Last Goodbye: The Strange Case of Terminal Lucidity. Scientific American Blog entry November 2014. https://blogs.scientificamerican.com/bering-in-mind/one-last-goodbye-the-strange-case-of-terminal-lucidity/ . Accessed on December 9, 2019.

Blofeld J. *Zen Teachings of Huang Po.* New York, NY: Grove Press; 1994.

Bouchard T. J., Lykken D. T., McGue M., Segal N. L., and Tellegen A. Sources of Human Psychological Differences: The Minnesota Study of Twins Reared Apart. Science, *250*, October 12, 1990. Online at http://web.missouri.edu/~segerti/1000H/Bouchard.pdf . Accessed on February 19, 2020.

Bullock P. Many Genes Influence Same-Sex Sexuality, Not a Single 'Gay Gene'. New York Times, August 29, 2019.

Buswell R. E., Jr., and Lopez D. S., Jr. Available at https://tricycle.org/magazine/10-misconceptions-about-buddhism/ . Accessed on November 23, 2019.

Campbell T. C. and Campbell T. M. *The China Study.* Dallas, TX: Benbella Books; 2004.

Carey B. Can We Really Inherit Trauma? New York Times, December 10, 2018.

Carroll S. Even Physicists Don't Understand Quantum Mechanics. New York Times, September 7, 2019.

Carroll S. *Something Deeply Hidden: Quantum Worlds and the Emergence of Spacetime.* New York, NY: Dutton; 2019.

Carroll S. His online blog at http://www.preposterousuniverse.com/blog/. There his gist of reality is succinctly stated in the upper right hand corner. Accessed on December 25, 2019.

Cepelewicz J. New Turmoil Over Predicting the Effects of Genes. *Quantamagazine: Genomics.* April 23, 2019. Available at https://www.quantamagazine.org/new-turmoil-over-predicting-the-effects-of-genes-20190423/ . Accessed on February 19, 2020.

Christopher T. 2017b. Science's Big Problem, Reincarnation's Big Potential, and Buddhists' Profound Embarrassment. Available online at http://www.mdpi.com/2077-1444/8/8/155 . Accessed on November 11, 2019.

Christopher T. 2017a. *A Hole in Science: An Opening for an Alternative Understanding of Life (Expanded Third Edition)*. Available at a number of online book retailers.

Christopher T. 2018. The Heritability Challenge to Evolution and Materialism: An Opening for Religious Perspectives. Open Journal of Philosophy 8(4): 355-364. 2018. Available online at https://www.scirp.org/Journal/paperinformation.aspx?paperid=86515. Accessed on November 11, 2019.

Collins F. *The Language of Life: DNA and the Revolution in Personalized Medicine*. New York, NY: HarperCollins; 2010.

Croston R., Branch C. L., Kozlovsky D. Y., Dukas R., and Pravosudov V. V. Heritability and Evolution of Cognitive Traits. *Behavioral Ecology*, 26(6), 1147-1459, 2015.

Dennett D. C. *From Bacteria to Bach: The Evolution of Minds*. New York, NY: W.W. Norton and Company; 2018.

Denworth L. The Kids Are Alright. *Scientific American*, September 2012. The article misses the obvious - that is that the purported ill-effects of social media usage could be largely redundant with the other ill-effects of hyper cell phone usage. Distinguishing relatively small problems associated social media usage is no relief if the alternative is simply being otherwise preoccupied with your cellphone.

Diamond J. *The World Until Yesterday*. New York, NY: Penguin Books; 2013.

Flynn J. R. Thinking in More Sophisticated Ways. *New York Times*, February 27, 2012.

Folger, T. Can We Keep Getting Smarter? *Scientific American*, September 2012.

Fromme P. and Spence J. C. H. Split Second Reactions. *Scientific American*, May 2017.

Gober M. *An End to Upside Down Thinking*. Cardiff-by-the-Sea, CA: Waterside Press; 2018.

Goldin I. Testing Times for Optimism. *Nature* vol. 554, February 22, 2018.

Goldstein D. San Francisco Had An Ambitious Plan to Tackle School Segregation. It Made It Worse. *New York Times*, April 25, 2019. Note the many critical comments from parents and teachers in the Reader Picks.

Goldstein J.S., Qvist S.A., Pinker S. Nuclear Power Can Save the World. *New York Times*, April 6, 2019.

Gorman J. Why Are These Foxes Tame? Maybe They Weren't So Wild to Begin With. *New York Times*, December 3, 2019. The article suggests that the experimental Siberian foxes may have in fact been originally from Canadian fox farms, and possibly not so wild after all.

Gottfredson L. S. The World Grows More Complex. *New York Times*, February 27, 2012.

Green E. D. Human Genome, Then and Now. *New York Times*, April 15, 2013.

Hall S. S. Revolution Postponed. *Scientific American*, October 2010.

Harris J. R. *No Two Alike*. New York, NY: W. W. Norton & Company; 2006.

Harris S. *Waking Up*. New York, NY: Simon & Schuster; 2014.

Hopkins W. D., Russell J. L., and Schaeffer J. Chimpanzee intelligence is heritable. *Current Biology*, 24:1649-1652, 2014.

Horgan J. Quest for Intelligence Genes Churns Out More Dubious Results. Available online at //blogs.scientificamerican.com/cross-check/2014/10/14/quest-for-intelligence-genes-churns-out-more-dubious-results/ Accessed on November 9, 2019.

Hossenfelder S. and McGaugh S. S. Is Dark Matter Real? *Scientific American*, August 2018.

IPBES Global Assessment Summary for Policymakers. Available online at https://ipbes.net/news/ipbes-global-assessment-summary-policy-makers-pdf . Accessed on November 21, 2019.

Iwasaki/Kapleau. Yaeko Iwasaki's Enlightenment Letters to Harada-Roshi and his Comments. In addition to *Three Pillars of Zen* it also found available at https://sites.google.com/site/esabsnichtenglisch/yaeko-iwasaki-s-enlightenment-letters-to-harada-roshi-and-his-comments . Accessed on November 3, 2019.

Jainworld. Spiritual Progress (Gunashtan). Available online at https://jainworld.com/philosophy/spiritual-progress-gunashtan/ . Accessed on December 30, 2019.

Kadin A. Fundamental Waves and the Reunification of Physics. Available online at https://fqxi.org/community/forum/topic/2972 . Accessed on December 25, 2019.

Kapleau P. *Three Pillars of Zen: Teaching, Practice, and Enlightenment.* Garden City, NY: Anchor Books; 1980.

Kingsley D. M. From Atoms to Traits. *Scientific American,* January 2009.

Kolata G. Live Long? Die Young? Answer Isn't Just in Genes. *New York Times,* August 31, 2006.

Kunsang E.M. Mixing Fire and Water: An Interview With Tulku Urgyen Rinpoche. Available online at http://levekunst.com/mixing-fire-and-water-an-interview-with-tulku-urgyen-rinpoche/. Accessed on December 24, 2019.

Landau E. Born in male body, Jenny knew early that she was a girl. CNN, June 14, 2009. Available at www.cnn.com/2009/HEALTH/06/12/sex.change.gender.transition/ Accessed on December 9, 2019.

Latham J. and Wilson A. The Great DNA Data Deficit: Are Genes for Disease a Mirage? Available at www.independentsciencenews.org/health/the-great-dna-data-deficit/ . Accessed on December 9, 2018.

Lee J. J., and 79 more authors/contributors. Gene discovery and polygenic prediction from a 1.1 million-person GWAS of educational attainment. *Nature Genetics* 50, 2018, pp. 1112-1121. Available at https://scholar.harvard.edu/files/laibson/files/ssgac_nature-genetics_072318.pdf . Accessed on February 19, 2020.

Leininger B., Leininger A., and Gross K. *Soul Survivor - The Reincarnation of a World War II Fighter Pilot.* New York, NY: Grand Central Publishing;

2009. A remarkable investigation motivated by a parent trying to disprove the apparent transcendental connection.

Lello L., Avery S. G., Tellier L., Vazquez A. I., de los Campos G., and Hsu S. D. H. Accurate Genomic Prediction of Human Height. *Genetics* Vol. 210, pp.477-497. Available online at https://www.genetics.org/content/210/2/477 . Accessed on February 19, 2020.

Lewin R. Is Your Brain Really Necessary? *Science*, Vol. 210, December 12, 1980. Available at www.rifters.com/real/articles/Science_No-Brain.pdf . Accessed on November 9, 2019.

Lopez D. S. Six Episodes in Buddhism and Science. Available at https://www.press.uchicago.edu/Misc/Chicago/493121.html . Accessed on December 9, 2019.

Luhrmann T. M. Beyond the Brain. *The Wilson Quarterly*, Summer 2012:28-34.

Lusseyran J. *And There Was Light*. Novato, CA: New World Library; 2014.

Malkus N. The Importance of Boots on the Ground in Schools. U.S. News and World Reports, March 3, 2018. Available at https://www.usnews.com/opinion/knowledge-bank/articles/2018-03-07/listen-to-teachers-to-avoid-graduation-scandals-like-dc-public-schools . Accessed on November 22, 2019.

Mattheissen P. *Nine-Headed Dragon River: Zen Journals 1969-1982*. Boulder, CO: Shambhala Publications; 1998.

Mayer E. L. *Extraordinary Knowing: Science, Skepticism, and the Inexplicable Powers of the Human Mind*. New York, NY: Bantom Books; 2007.

Mayr E. *What Evolution Is*. New York, NY: Basic Books; 2001.

McCarthy M. Mukherjee follows cancer best seller with 'The Gene'. Available online at www.usatoday.com/story/life/books/2016/05/19/the-gene-an-intimate-history-siddhartha-mukherjee-book-review/84201180 Accessed on September 14, 2017.

MacFarquhar L. Last Call. *The New Yorker*, June 24, 2013. Available online at www.newyorker.com/magazine/2013/06/24/last-call-3. Accessed on December 9, 2019.

McGaugh J. L. and LePort A. Remembrance of All Things Past. *Scientific American,* February 2014.

McGee K. What Really Happened At The School Where Every Graduate Got Into College. *NPR.* November 28, 2017. Available at https://www.npr.org/sections/ed/2017/11/28/564054556/what-really-happened-at-the-school-where-every-senior-got-into-college . Accessed on December 9, 2019.

Mozaffarian D. and Glickman G. Our Food Is Killing Too Many of Us. *New York Times,* August 26, 2019.

Mukherjee S. *The Gene: An Intimate History.* New York, NY: Scribner; 2016.

Nagel T. The Core of 'Mind and Cosmos'. *New York Times,* August 18, 2013.

Nestler E. J. Hidden Switches in the Mind. *Scientific American,* December 2011.

Nestler E. J. The Mind's Hidden Switches (podcast transcript) at www.scientificamerican.com/podcast/episode.cfm?id=the-minds-hidden-switches-11-11-22. Accessed on November 9, 2019.

Nisargadatta S. *I AM THAT.* Durham, NC: Acorn Press; 1973 (paperback printing 1999).

Olson K. R. When Sex and Gender Collide. *Scientific American,* September 2017.

Owens D. The Efficiency Dilemma. *The New Yorker,* December 12, 2010.

Padawer R. What's So Bad About a Boy Who Wants to Wear a Dress? *New York Times Magazine,* August 8, 2012.

Phelps S. M. and Wedow R. What Genetics Is Teaching Us About Sexuality. *New York Times,* August 29, 2019.

Pinker S. *How the Mind Works.* New York, NY: W. W. Norton; 1997.

Pinker S. *Blank Slate: The Modern Denial of Human Nature.* New York, NY: Viking; 2002.

Pinker S. *The Better Angels of Our Nature - Why Violence has Declined*. New York, NY: Penguin Books; 2011.

Pinker S. Science Is Not Your Enemy. *The New Republic*, August 6, 2013.

Pinker S. *Enlightenment Now: The Case For Reason, Science, Humanism, and Progress*. New York, NY: Viking; 2018.

Plomin R. and von Stumm S. The new genetics of intelligence. *Nature Reviews | Genetics*. 2018:19, pp. 148-159. Available at https://www.gwern.net/docs/iq/2018-plomin.pdf . Accessed on February 19, 2020.

Pollyanna. An Amazon reader review for the *The Big Picture* which was submitted on June 20, 2016 by a reader named "Alex".

Raichlen D.A. and Alexander G.E. Why Your Brain Needs Exercise. *Scientific American*, January 2020.

Radin D. *Real Magic: Ancient Wisdom, Modern Science, and a Guide to the Secret Power of the Universe*. New York, NY: Harmony Books; 2018.

Richard. J. L., Lutz A., and Davidson R. J. mind of the meditator. *Scientific American*, November 2014.

Schafer A. Relatedness. Available online at https://genetics.thetech.org/ask/ask166. Accessed on November 9, 2019.

Shapiro E. (1) Only 7 Black Students Got Into Stuyvesant, NY's Most Selective High School, Out of 895 Spots. *New York Times*, March 18, 2019. Note the scale of the rebuttal comments starting with Reader Picks.

Shapiro E. (2) Why Some of the Country's Best Urban Schools Are Facing a Reckoning. *New York Times*, July 5, 2019. Note teacher comments starting with the first one in Reader Picks.

Shaw J. Is Epigenetics Inherited? Harvard Magazine, 2017. Available online at http://www.harvardmag.com/pdf/2017/05-pdfs/0517-13.pdf . Accessed on January 4, 2020.

Sheldrake R. and Wolpert L. (Sheldrake bet) The Genome Wager. Available online at www.sheldrake.org/reactions/the-genome-wager. Accessed on November 9, 2019.

Sheldrake R. (2012a) *The Presence of the Past*. Rochester, VT: Park Street Press; 2012.

Sheldrake R. (2012b) *Science Set Free: 10 Paths to New Discovery*. New York, NY: Deepak Chopra Books; 2012.

Sheldrake R. *Dogs That Know When Their Owners Are Coming Home: Fully Revised and Updated*. New York, NY: Broadway Books; 2011.

Shermer M. *Heavens on Earth: The Scientific Search for the Afterlife, Immortality, and Utopia*. New York, NY: St. Martin's Griffen; 2018.

Shermer M. Kids These Days. *Scientific American*, December 2018. Available at https://michaelshermer.com/2018/12/kids-these-days-how-to-avert-looming-crisis/ . Accessed on December 9, 2019.

Simon D. 10 Most Powerful Production Motorcycles 2018. Bike Stop, July 7 2018. Available at https://www.bikestop.co.uk/blog/top-10-most-powerful-production-motorcycles-2018 . Accessed on November 22, 2019.

Sludge. An Amazon reader review for the *The Gene* which was submitted on June 5, 2018 by a reader named "Earnest Sludge".

Smil V. Global Population and the Nitrogen Cycle. *Scientific American*, July 1997.

Smil V. Revolution? More Like a Crawl. *Politico*, May 2015. Available at vaclavsmil.com .

Smil V. *Harvesting theBiosphere: What We Have Taken From Nature*. Cambridge, MA: MIT Press; 2015.

Smil V. Energy transitions, renewables and rational energy use: A reality check. *IEEE Spectrum*, November 2015. Available at vaclavsmil.com .

Smil V. Examining energy transitions: a dozen insights based on performance. Energy Research & Social Science 22 (2016) 194-197. Available at vaclavsmil.com .

Smil V. *Addio* to the Mediterranean Diet. *IEEE Spectrum*, September 2016. Available at vaclavsmil.com .

Smil V. (Chase). Mountains and Molehills (JPMorgan Energy Issue, March 2019). Available at Vaclav Smil's website (vaclavsmil.com) .

Sohail M., Maier R. M., Ganna A., Bloemendal A., Martin A. R., Turchin M. C., Chiang C. WK, Hirschhorn J., Daly M. J., Patterson N., Neale B., Mathieson I., Reich D., and Sunyaev S. R. Polygenic adaptation on height is overestimated due to uncorrected uncorrected stratification in genome wide association studies. *eLife*. March 21, 2019. Available at https://reich.hms.harvard.edu/sites/reich.hms.harvard.edu/files/inline-files/2019_SohailMaier_eLife_Height.pdf . Accessed on February 19, 2020.

Solomon A. *Far From the Tree*. New York, NY: Scribner; 2012.

Sowell T. *Black Rednecks and White Liberals*. New York, NY: Encounter Books; 2006.

Spellmeyer K. After the Future. *Tricycle*. Fall 2015.

Stoklosa D. Every Car With at Least 700 Horsepower You Can Buy Today. Car and Driver, September 4, 2018. Available at https://www.msn.com/en-us/autos/research/every-car-with-at-least-700-horsepower-you-can-buy-today/ . Accessed on November 22, 2019.

Tart C. T. *The End of Materialism*. Oakland, CA: New Harbinger Publications; 2009.

Treffert D. A. *Islands of Genius*. London, UK: Jessica Kingsley Publishers; 2010.

Trut L. and Dugatkin L. E. How to Build a Dog. *Scientific American*, May 2017.

UCS Nuclear. https://www.ucsusa.org/resources/nuclear-power-global-warming. Accessed on December 23, 2019.

Venter, J. C. *A Life Decoded: My Genome: My Life*. New York, NY: Viking Adult: 2007. An apt retrospective title here would be *My Science-Based Fantasy Life*.

Voosen/Smil. Meet Vaclav Smil, the man who quietly shaped how the world thinks about energy. *Science*. March 21, 2018. Available online at https://www.sciencemag.org/news/2018/03/meet-vaclav-smil-man-who-has-quietly-shaped-how-world-thinks-about-energy . Accessed on November 21, 2019.

Wade N. A Dissenting Voice as the Genome is Sifted to Fight Disease. *New York Times*, September 16, 2008.

Watson J. D. A Conversation With James D. Watson. *Scientific American*, April 2003.

Watson J. D. with Berry A. and Davies K. *DNA: The Story of the Genetic Revolution*. New York, NY: Albert A. Knopf; 2017.

Williams W. Blind to Real Problems. Available at https://www.creators.com/read/walter-williams/06/18/blind-to-real-problems . Accessed on November 22, 2019.

Williams W. Cruelty to Black Students. Available at https://www.creators.com/read/walter-williams/09/16/cruelty-to-black-students . Accessed on November 22, 2019.

Williams W. Higher Education in America. Available at https://www.creators.com/read/walter-williams/05/19/higher-education-in-america . Accessed on December 9, 2019.

Williams W. Black Education Decline. Available at https://www.creators.com/read/walter-williams/06/19/black-education-decline . Accessed on November 22, 2019.

Williams W. Discrimination and Disparities. Available at https://www.creators.com/read/walter-williams/05/19/discrimination-and-disparities-42130 . Accessed on November 22, 2019.

Williams W. Who Are the Racists? Available at https://www.creators.com/read/walter-williams/11/19/who-are-the-racists. Accessed on December 8, 2019.

Yong E. Psychology's Replication Crisis Can't Be Wished Away. Atlantic March 4, 2016. Available online at https://www.theatlantic.com/science/archive/2016/03/psychologys-replication-crisis-cant-be-wished-away/472272/ . Accessed on September 13, 2017.

Young A. I. Solving the missing heritability problem. *PLOS | Genetics*. June 24, 2019. Available at https://journals.plos.org/plosgenetics/article?id=10.1371/journal.pgen.1008222 . Accessed on February 19, 2020.

Yuste R. and Church G. M. The New Century of the Brain. *Scientific American*, March 2014.

Zimmer C. Is Most of Our DNA Garbage? *New York Times Magazine*, March 8, 2015.

www.ingramcontent.com/pod-product-compliance
Lightning Source LLC
Chambersburg PA
CBHW060525080526
44586CB00012B/615